Chapter One

TRANSFORMING LIFE FROM WITHIN

Kingdom Power

THE KINGDOM OF GOD IS AT HAND.

It's a phrase we've all heard at one time or another. It's a phrase you are probably familiar with or have heard in a sermon. It's a phrase I have used while preaching and a phrase that I find great meaning in. Jesus began His earthly ministry with this phrase (Mark 1:15). In so doing, Jesus made clear the foundational truth upon which He would serve, give His life, and rise again. But what does it mean for the kingdom of God to be at hand? And what *is* the kingdom of God as well?

The term *kingdom* refers to a rule or authority. The kingdom of God refers to God's rule or authority—that is, a sphere of divine jurisdiction from which He reigns. We know it as the "kingdom of God" when it is referencing a Person. We know it as the "kingdom of heaven" when referencing a location. But in both cases, it refers to the sphere of God's jurisdiction and rule. God is the Ruler of His kingdom. Absolutely nothing sits outside of God's comprehensive kingdom rule. Each of us sits beneath His rule, governed by Him. Believers have been chosen by Him to help advance His kingdom's agenda. The kingdom agenda can be defined as the visible manifestation of the comprehensive rule of God over every area of life. When you and I choose to live according to God's kingdom rule and agenda, we receive empowerment from on high. We receive the tools and the resources we need in order to accomplish His rule. As any great ruler or king would do, God provides for and supplies those who promote His kingdom's priorities and goals.

When you and I choose to live according to God's kingdom rule and agenda, we receive empowerment from on high.

Now that we understand the kingdom and God's rule, what does it mean for the kingdom of God to be at hand?

UNLEASHED

Releasing God's Glorious Kingdom in and Through You

Tony Evans

W Publishing Group
An Imprint of Thomas Nelson

Unleashed

Published by W Publishing, an imprint of Thomas Nelson, 501 Nelson Place, Nashville, TN 37214, USA.

ISBN 978-1-4003-4245-7 (audiobook)
ISBN 978-1-4003-4244-0 (ePub)
ISBN 978-1-4003-4959-3 (ITPE)
ISBN 978-1-4003-4240-2 (HC)

HarperCollins Publishers, Macken House, 39/40 Mayor Street Upper,
Dublin 1, D01 C9W8, Ireland (https://www.harpercollins.com)

Library of Congress Control Number: 2025935051

Printed in the United States of America

25 26 27 28 29 LBC 5 4 3 2 1

CONTENTS

For something to be at hand, it needs to be close enough to touch. Your hand is never more than a few feet from your body. Even if you were to stretch your hand as far as you possibly could, it would still be near enough to see and use. For the kingdom of God to be at hand means that God's kingdom—His rule, power, and authority—are within close proximity to each of us. When Jesus Christ came to Earth and sojourned on our planet, He brought the kingdom near to us all. Upon His resurrection, He left the Holy Spirit so the kingdom of God and all it contains would always be accessible and close by.

If you picked up this book because you are hoping to unleash the power of God throughout every area of your life, the first thing you must know is that this comes through a conscious, intentional alignment underneath His rule. When you live in alignment under God and His rule, His kingdom power is at hand. His kingdom authority is at hand. God's kingdom favor is at hand. He is near enough for you to tap into all He has to offer you.

DISCOVERING THE POWER WITHIN REACH

When England's monarch travels to one of the many castles throughout the United Kingdom, the royal standard is flown at that location to indicate the king's presence. This flag is raised in order to make it clearly known that the ruler is situated there.

The question I need to ask you as we start our journey

together is, What flag flies over your life? Is there a clear indication that the King is at hand and has arrived to abide within you? Has the King made His presence known in the place of your heart and soul, where He can rule? The answers to those questions will make all the difference in how much of God's power, healing, favor, blessing, peace, and authority is unleashed in your life.

God's kingdom and His agenda must be prioritized for His power to be actualized in and through you. Jesus made it a point to emphasize the kingdom of God throughout His earthly ministry. Not only that, but we also see He made it a point to emphasize the kingdom of God when He returned following His resurrection. If you turn to the book of Acts, you'll quickly see that it was written by a physician named Luke. Luke is also the author of the gospel of Luke. In Acts, though, Luke was writing to a man named Theophilus, who had helped fund Luke's research. As a researcher and physician, Luke wrote in a very detailed way. He is the one who told us that forty days elapsed between the time of Jesus' resurrection and the time of His ascension to heaven. He also told us that, in these forty days, Jesus taught on the kingdom of God. We read in the opening verses of the book of Acts:

> In my former book, Theophilus, I wrote about all that Jesus began to do and to teach until the day he was taken up to heaven, after giving instructions through the Holy Spirit to the apostles he had chosen. After his suffering, he presented himself to them and gave many convincing

> proofs that he was alive. He appeared to them over a period of forty days and spoke about the kingdom of God. (Acts 1:1–3 NIV)

The subject of the kingdom of God was so important to Jesus during His earthly ministry and forty-day return after His resurrection that He prioritized it in His communication. And yet understanding and applying kingdom principles has only recently become a more widely known focus in our contemporary Christian culture. I recall when I first wrote my book *The Kingdom Agenda* in the 1990s, the subject was much more distant to mainstream Christian thought and application. The terms *kingdom* and *agenda* were perceived to be somewhat abrasive, so much so that the publisher sought to have me title the book something more "popular." That's why my first edition in 1997 was titled *What a Way to Live: Running All of Life by God's Kingdom Agenda*. But since Jesus made the kingdom of God His priority while on earth in what He spoke about and taught, I sought to re-title my book *The Kingdom Agenda* when I rereleased it with a different publisher a few years later. It's been in print under that title ever since.

Today, thankfully, contemporary Christian thought and language have caught on to the emphasis of the kingdom and even God's kingdom agenda. In fact, the subject of the kingdom is frequently preached about, written about, and sung about today. I'm very happy to have seen this change take place over the past three decades. Without the kingdom, we lack the biblical-historical context for Christ's mission.

The kingdom is also the thread that holds the entirety of Scripture together in a thematic tie.

LIVING UNDER DIVINE AUTHORITY

If you've done any formal training in studying Scripture, you know that the subject of systematic theology concerns itself with the organization of biblical truth and principles within structures. Since certain subjects are spread throughout the Bible, the process of systematic theology sets out to study these subjects in all areas of their appearance.

This might be compared to a subject index in a book. In a subject index the reader is able to look up a certain topic and see all the pages on which this subject appears in the book. That way the reader can go to one of these pages and see all the content on that subject that there is, and then compare it with the other pages on which the subject shows up. Similarly, in systematic theology, theologians study, organize, and structure subjects as they appear throughout the Bible. Thus, if you want to learn more on the attributes of God, for example, or ecclesiology (the study of the church), you study all of the places these subjects appear.

Now, biblical theology differs from systematic theology. I gave you insight into systematic theology so you could have a reference point for biblical theology. Biblical theology does not concern itself with pulling everything together as it appears throughout the entire Bible. Rather, biblical theology concerns itself with what a specific author said to a specific group of people at a specific time around a specific subject. Biblical theology is a narrower study approach than systematic theology. The reason why biblical theology is important is because it allows you to see what is being emphasized at a certain time on a certain subject by a certain author and in a certain book.

Let's do a brief bibliocentric-theological analysis of the book of Acts as it relates to the subject of the kingdom of God. As we do so, we will uncover Luke's emphasis to Theophilus and his other intended readers. For example, in addition to Acts 1:3, the following passages in Acts speak on the subject of the kingdom:

> But when they believed Philip preaching the good news about the kingdom of God and the name of Jesus Christ, they were being baptized, men and women alike. (8:12)

> And he entered the synagogue and continued speaking out boldly for three months, reasoning and persuading them about the kingdom of God. (19:8)

> "And now, behold, I know that all of you, among whom I went about preaching the kingdom, will no longer see my face." (20:25)

> When they had set a day for Paul, they came to him at his lodging in large numbers; and he was explaining to them by solemnly testifying about the kingdom of God and trying to persuade them concerning Jesus, from both

> the Law of Moses and from the Prophets, from morning until evening. (28:23)

> And he stayed two full years in his own rented quarters and was welcoming all who came to him, preaching the kingdom of God and teaching concerning the Lord Jesus Christ with all openness, unhindered. (28:30–31)

What we can determine by looking at these passages together is that from a biblical-theological framework it is absolutely clear that the teaching on the kingdom of God, which Jesus did for the forty days between His resurrection and His ascension, struck a chord in the apostles' hearts, minds, souls, and ministry. We know this because they kept the theme going throughout the book of Acts, during the time of the establishment of the church.

The concept of the kingdom of God is not merely based on verses from Acts but on other passages as well; it is the abiding theme of Scripture, the abiding message of Jesus Christ, and the abiding subject of the apostles in the New Testament. The kingdom is the theme of God's purpose in history. It is the theme of God's sphere of jurisdiction and the place of His rule. The kingdom is God's agenda.

The reason why Jesus taught so comprehensively and consistently on the kingdom of God is so that His followers would carry on this teaching. He wanted them to understand the governance of God's jurisdiction. In this way, if ever there was errant thinking, ideas, or philosophies—or even errant social orientations—His followers would have a standard by which to measure these ideas. They would have a truth filter through which to evaluate and respond to the world's strategies and ways of thought. Without a standard, we are prone to wander. And when we wander, we no longer tap into the power, authority, peace, and favor of God Himself through Jesus Christ, His Son.

Scripture explains how each of us as followers of Jesus have been transferred out of the kingdom of darkness and into the kingdom of Christ. You once dwelt in a dark, evil, and secular kingdom. But once you have trusted in Jesus for the forgiveness of your sins, you no longer dwell there. Colossians 1:13–14 states, "For He rescued us from the domain of darkness, and transferred us to the kingdom of His beloved Son, in whom we have redemption, the forgiveness of sins."

Many of you reading this book have visited Disney World at one point or another. It's often called the Magic Kingdom or "The Happiest Place on Earth." They try to make Disney World, the Magic Kingdom, full of fun, frivolity, food, and festivities. My late wife, Lois, and I took our kids there when they were growing up. It was a nice place to visit. But it was not where we lived. For starters, no one could afford to live at Disney World. Visitors often wear T-shirts that read "The Most Expensive Day on Earth" when they attend because of the cost. But another reason why it's not home is because it is not set up to be home. It is set up to keep you entertained and intoxicated on fun for the time you are there in the hope that you will lose sight of the fact that this is not reality.

Like Disney World, our present world seeks to deceive

When you make your decisions on where or how to invest your time, talents, and treasures, you need to do so based on a kingdom worldview, not a worldly wisdom.

you into thinking that where you are and what you do is the sum total of who you are and is all you need to focus on. What the world wants to do is create an impression on you that it is reality. Yet that's just not true. The world is its own kingdom that seeks to leave God out. The world is antithetical to the jurisdiction of the rule of God.

The kingdom of God is your reality. Thus, when you make your decisions on where or how to invest your time, talents, and treasures, you need to do so based on a kingdom worldview, not a worldly wisdom. When you were saved, hopefully you were baptized. To be baptized is to signify living under a new jurisdiction. It is to signify having been put into a new family, realm, or sphere of dominance. To be baptized as a follower of Jesus Christ means you belong to a new order. You live in this world, but you are now informed by another—the kingdom of God.

ACCESSING HEAVEN'S RESOURCES FOR YOUR LIFE

Acknowledging the kingdom of God as your reality is crucial to understanding how to unleash God's power in your life. Just as you would function and operate under the rules and policies of a new corporation or business should you change jobs, when you change kingdoms, you are to function and operate under the rules of God's kingdom.

Think back to when you were in school. If you ever moved or changed schools or even colleges, you understood clearly that you wouldn't have been able to function at your new school based on your previous school's rules or handbook. Regardless of what had been true in the old school, that no longer carried authority and weight in the new one. You were under new leadership and new rules. Similarly, under God's rule and in His kingdom, you are to follow His lead. You are to no longer live by the world's standards.

Satan and his world order want to keep you so distracted, obsessed, entertained, or addicted that you forget you no longer work for them or live within their rule. Satan wants you to function by his rules. But now that you are a citizen of the heavenly kingdom, you are released from Satan's rule over you. Satan's only power is through deception. He has no true authority over you at all. We read about this in Colossians 2:15:

> When He [Jesus] had disarmed the rulers and authorities, He made a public display of them, having triumphed over them through Him.

Jesus disarmed Satan and his fallen angels through His death and resurrection. Yet Satan doesn't want you to realize that, so he will try anything to get you to still function in his world.

The way you and I can unleash God's kingdom power and favor in our lives begins with the realization of the kingdom itself. Orienting yourself to a kingdom worldview will help you manifest the power of God both in and through you. The primary way you can orient your thoughts and worldview to God's perspective comes through an abiding relationship with Jesus and the presence of His Holy Spirit. The job of the Spirit is to bring the reality of the new jurisdiction into your experience (Romans 14:17).

As you draw closer to the Spirit and seek a greater intimacy with Him, you begin to see things with new eyes. You begin to see through the lies and deceit of this world as you discern the truth with spiritual sight. Romans 12:1–2 describes this transformational process:

> Therefore I urge you, brethren, by the mercies of God, to present your bodies a living and holy sacrifice, acceptable to God, which is your spiritual service of worship. And do not be conformed to this world, but be transformed by the renewing of your mind, so that you may prove what the will of God is, that which is good and acceptable and perfect.

Jesus returned to heaven after His resurrection, and when He did, He sent the Holy Spirit to be present with each of us. The Holy Spirit's role is to transform each of us into the likeness of Christ. We also see this in Romans 8:26–29:

> In the same way the Spirit also helps our weakness; for we do not know how to pray as we should, but the Spirit Himself intercedes for us with groanings too deep for words; and He who searches the hearts knows what the mind of the Spirit is, because He intercedes for the saints according to the will of God.
>
> And we know that God causes all things to work together for good to those who love God, to those who

> are called according to His purpose. For those whom He foreknew, He also predestined to become conformed to the image of His Son, so that He would be the firstborn among many brethren.

It's the Holy Spirit's role to transform us into the likeness of Jesus, and He does this through a number of ways. He transforms our thoughts, our emotions, and much more. This is why we read in Acts 1 that the disciples were not to leave and do the work of God until they received the Spirit's power. It says in Acts 1:6–8,

> So when they had come together, they were asking Him, saying, "Lord, is it at this time You are restoring the kingdom to Israel?" He said to them, "It is not for you to know times or epochs which the Father has fixed by His own authority; but you will receive power when the Holy Spirit has come upon you; and you shall be My witnesses both in Jerusalem, and in all Judea and Samaria, and even to the remotest part of the earth."

The Holy Spirit is the continuation of the work of Jesus on earth. When Jesus left, He told His disciples He would send them the Helper, who would assist them in their work (John 15:26–27). This Helper is the Spirit within each of us. His purpose is to unleash the kingdom's work in the lives of kingdom people.

Most of us have electricity in our homes, which means we have power. Your appliances only work because of the power of electricity. Your lights come on because of the power of electricity. You heat your home and cook your food due to the power of electricity. You cool your home in the summer because of the power of electricity. You are, in many ways, attached to power. If there is a power outage, you know it and feel it in many ways. This is because power unleashes you to carry on much of your everyday life.

Now, just because you have access to power doesn't mean you will use it. It is only when you turn on the power by turning on a power switch or plugging in an appliance that you access and use the power. Experiencing the benefits of power is tied to your use of that power, not merely the presence of power itself. While the Spirit's power is guaranteed, it is not automatic.

THE ROLE OF THE SPIRIT IN KINGDOM LIVING

If you have come to Jesus Christ and are saved, you have the Holy Spirit's power accessible to you. But that power will not be forced on you. Just like a refrigerator won't run if it's not plugged into a power source, neither will you unleash God's kingdom power in your life if you do not plug into the Holy Spirit. The presence of spiritual power does not automatically equate to the use of spiritual power. This use is unleashed through your access point with the Spirit. Just like many heating systems require an igniter to start the heat flowing throughout a home or office, God has given every believer an igniter to get into the kingdom power He has for each of us. But if the Holy Spirit is not free to ignite His power in your life, the spiritual authority, peace, favor, and blessings will not be realized or occur for you. In John 16:5–7, 12–15, Jesus explained the Spirit's role more fully:

> "But now I am going to Him who sent Me; and none of you asks Me, 'Where are You going?' But because I have said these things to you, sorrow has filled your heart. But I tell you the truth, it is to your advantage that I go away; for if I do not go away, the Helper will not come to you; but if I go, I will send Him to you. . . .
>
> "I have many more things to say to you, but you cannot bear them now. But when He, the Spirit of truth, comes, He will guide you into all the truth; for He will not speak on His own initiative, but whatever He hears, He will speak; and He will disclose to you what is to come. He will glorify Me, for He will take of Mine and will disclose it to you. All things that the Father has are Mine; therefore I said that He takes of Mine and will disclose it to you."

God has given every believer an access line of disclosure and communication. The Holy Spirit translates the thoughts and will of God to each of us who abide in Christ. He discloses truth to us. In today's terms you might think of it like a direct message or text. It is our own personal connection so that we can communicate with and hear the mind of God. The Holy Spirit has been gifted as a divine GPS (global positioning system) at work in our lives. You and I can live in sync with God when we are in sync with His Spirit. He reveals the truth we need to know. He reveals the direction we are to take. He unveils the wisdom we are to base our decisions on. He gives us God's perspective and kingdom worldview.

We live in a day when far too many Christians are being culturalized rather than kingdomized. Too many Christians are buying into secular thinking rather than spiritual truth based on God's Word. A virus has been released in order to try to trip us up. This virus is called worldly wisdom. It includes what your friends may say or think. It includes what the media and social influencers may push you to believe. It includes the way of thinking that aligns with Satan's world order. This virus has caused mass destruction in so many lives and throughout our world. The only effective antivirus software available is the truth of the Word of God made known through the Spirit.

We live in a day when far too many Christians are being culturalized rather than kingdomized.

The power of the Spirit is tied to the teaching of the kingdom and the revealed Word of God. It is only when you embrace this truth and live as a kingdom disciple that you will unleash the full experience of God and His will in your life. You cannot expect to hear from Jesus through the power of the Spirit when you refuse to live under the jurisdiction of the King and His kingdom.

If you try to bring the kingdom into the culture or the

culture into the kingdom, you have compromised the kingdom values of God. Just like a little arsenic will spoil an entire pot of stew, even a little of the world's wisdom will defile the truth of God and its power to work in your life. Compromising your views or perspectives doesn't shortchange anyone else but you. You will gain full access to God's power through one access point only: the kingdom of God and your alignment under God in it.

The moment the kingdom of this culture goes against the kingdom of God and you side with the culture, you have unplugged yourself from the power source of your highest good. It is up to you to decide how much of God's power you want in your life. He has made the process clear throughout His Word.

When government agencies want to teach their agents how to spot counterfeit money, they don't teach them by showing them counterfeit money. Rather, they teach them by showing them authentic currency. They get them so fully acquainted with the authentic currency that the agents can easily recognize any deviation when they see it. The culture is offering Christians a counterfeit power. It may look like the real deal. It may feel like the real deal. It may even smell like the real deal. But it's fake. And fake power is worth nothing. God wants you to become so familiar and acquainted with His kingdom agenda and His kingdom worldview that you can spot the errors, lies, and deceptions quickly and easily. He wants you to access authentic power rather than getting tripped up in a fake matrix of tricks, mirrors, and traps.

When you truly tap into the authentic power of God's

kingdom, you will see the Spirit of God manifesting God's will both in you and through you. You will become a witness to testify of the power of God. That is the way Jesus set up His kingdom to expand. It was never set up to expand through force or subjugation. Rather, the kingdom of Jesus Christ was to expand through the testimony and witness of His true followers.

CARRYING YOUR KINGDOM PASSPORT DAILY

I've been traveling overseas a lot as we film and prepare the story of *Unbound: The Bible's Journey Through History*. As I travel, I always bring my passport. This is because my passport identifies my citizenship. No matter where I go in the world, my passport declares that I belong to the United States. I may be in England, Germany, or Belgium, but I am only there to visit. I don't belong there long term. My passport reminds both me and them that those places are not my home. If I were to ever get into a bind or situation that required the US government's assistance, my passport would qualify me for that.

For the sake of illustration, you and I live in an earthly kingdom apart from the heavenly kingdom of God. Because we are made in the image of God, we have been issued passports from this heavenly kingdom. These passports grant us access to the kingdom authority granted to us through Jesus Christ in the heavenly realm (Ephesians 1:3). But unfortunately, today, too many Christians no longer travel with their kingdom passports. When they go to work, they leave their passport at home. When they hang out with their friends, they leave their passport at home. When they go on their social media channels to post or like posts, they leave their kingdom passport at home. And yet when they get into a bind, the first one they call is God. But without their access to His power through an alignment under His rule and abiding with His Son, Jesus Christ, through the Holy Spirit, they don't gain the help or favor they need. Functioning under kingdom alignment naturally activates the work of the Holy Spirit in your life.

There are many ways for you to unleash the power and blessing of God in your life. But like a runner in baseball trying to score at home plate, if you miss first base, the run won't count. You'll be out instead. First base is the kingdom of God. First base is your alignment under God's rule as the King of His kingdom. First base is an awareness and application of God's kingdom perspective.

In order for anything in the next chapters to make an impact in your life, you'll need to get this established first: God is to hold first place in your life. Matthew stated it best: "But seek first His kingdom and His righteousness, and all these things will be added to you" (6:33). The good news is that it shouldn't be too hard to seek first the kingdom and His righteousness, for the kingdom of God is at hand.

Chapter Two

EMPOWERED BY HEAVEN

Kingdom Authority

WHEN YOU BOARD AN AIRPLANE OR BOOK YOURSELF A FLIGHT, you are often given at least two ticket choices: coach or first class. Now, these two choices can come in a variety of names, such as economy, premium, or business class. Regardless of what they are called by the different airlines, they indicate a separation in seating. The seats near the front of the plane will cost you a significant amount more. For that additional cost, you'll get a larger seat and more personalized and upgraded service with regard to meals and drinks.

I fly a lot and have a lot of frequent-flier miles. I'll often upgrade myself or a traveling companion for free to the nicer seats. Yet no matter what section of the plane I sit in, one thing remains the same: I arrive at the same destination as everyone else on the plane. Both coach and first class always end up at the same place. The benefits of sitting in first class affect your journey, not your destination. The benefits make your journey far more pleasant and restful. But the destination is the same as everyone else's on the plane.

Similarly, for those who have trusted in Jesus Christ for the salvation of their sins, the destination is the same. We will all arrive in heaven one day due to the shed blood and sacrifice of Jesus. But the journey there—your earth story—can be a far different experience depending on whether you choose to upgrade your spiritual life or travel basic economy in coach. God has a lot of frequent spiritual miles and offers an upgrade to any of us who want it. He offers a better spiritual journey to every believer who wishes to function at another level of comfort, peace, and power. Now, keep in mind, it does not affect the destination of Christians. The destination of Christians is the same. But it does affect how you get there.

When you choose to upgrade your spiritual life according to the principles of Scripture—principles we will go over in this book—you'll unleash a greater level of kingdom authority in your life. *Kingdom authority* can be defined as the divinely authorized right and responsibility God bequeaths to believers in order for us to exercise and experience His rule and power while on earth.

Everyone who is saved for eternity does not experience

the same level of power from God. This is due to differing levels of kingdom commitment. Far too many believers fail to upgrade their spiritual lives simply because they are not operating in an authorized manner in which to receive the upgrade. God desires for each of us to gain access to the spiritual upgrade. In fact, He's designed each of us in a way so that we have the capacity for a spiritual upgrade. But He's not going to force His power or His authority on us.

SPOTTING FALSE RELIGION'S TRAP

One of the best illustrations of this principle of kingdom authority in Scripture shows up in Mark 11. It is a story we don't hear preached on very much. It's not a feel-good situation, and biblical stories like this one can leave people scratching their heads. The story doesn't fit our "Jesus mold" of how we envision Jesus to have behaved. But because it is in Scripture, we know it to be true. It shows us a different side of Jesus that is important to know about. He wasn't always walking around healing, hugging, and giving people hope. Jesus turned over tables when He got angry in the temple. He also cut short the life of a tree. Let's read about this latter event in Mark 11.

Shortly after crowds of people shouted "Hosanna" to Jesus and welcomed Him with full hearts of adoration as He rode on a donkey, Jesus left the city of Jerusalem. No doubt He expended a lot of energy in that emotion-filled ride on the donkey. He was hungry. We read:

> Jesus entered Jerusalem and came into the temple; and after looking around at everything, He left for Bethany with the twelve, since it was already late.
>
> On the next day, when they had left Bethany, He became hungry. Seeing at a distance a fig tree in leaf, He went to see if perhaps He would find anything on it; and when He came to it, He found nothing but leaves, for it was not the season for figs. He said to it, "May no one ever eat fruit from you again!" And His disciples were listening. (Mark 11:11–14)

In His humanity, it appears that Jesus may have been not only hungry but perhaps even *hangry*. After all, it wasn't the season for figs. But Jesus had spotted a fig tree with leaves on it, so His hopes rose. Leaves indicated the presence of fruit. Yet as He got closer to the tree, He realized the leaves had produced a false hope and there was no fruit at all. Frustrated by what He saw, Jesus spoke death to the tree, saying, "May no one ever eat fruit from you again!"

The passage tells us that the disciples were listening. I can imagine them listening like a child might when a parent gets frustrated. You may have seen this before. The child's eyes will get a little bigger as they listen more intently to try to find out the cause or source of frustration. The disciples didn't dare speak up at the time because they could sense Jesus' frustration. But they did listen.

I'm sure Jesus' harsh response, especially after such an emotional high in the city for all of them, was jarring. It provoked their attention. They may have wondered why He responded as He did. Surely it wasn't just about the tree. What the disciples were hearing in this situation was concerning the principle of false religion. False religion involves having the appearance, or external look, of religion but nothing real inside. That's what religion is on its own. The apostle Paul called it a "form of godliness." He described it like this when he warned believers to stay far away from people like that:

> But realize this, that in the last days difficult times will come. For men will be lovers of self, lovers of money, boastful, arrogant, revilers, disobedient to parents, ungrateful, unholy, unloving, irreconcilable, malicious gossips, without self-control, brutal, haters of good, treacherous, reckless, conceited, lovers of pleasure rather than lovers of God, holding to a form of godliness, although they have denied its power; Avoid such men as these. (2 Timothy 3:1–5)

Paul was describing people who look the part of Christianity and know how to carry their Bibles, wear their cross jewelry, or speak Christianese; but when you get close enough, you realize it's all for show. There's nothing authentic there. It's merely pomp and paraphernalia. Jesus used the example of the fig tree to teach His disciples about the emptiness of false religion. They had seen His hunger. They had seen His hopes rise as He walked to the leafed tree. Then they witnessed His disappointment when there was no fruit. What's more, a day later they witnessed the result of His statement to the tree. We read about this in Mark 11:19–22: "When evening came, they would go out of the city. As they were passing by in the morning, they saw the fig tree withered from the roots up. Being reminded, Peter said to Him, 'Rabbi, look, the fig tree which You cursed has withered.' And Jesus answered saying to them, 'Have faith in God.'"

In one short day the tree had experienced a reversal of fortune. What Jesus had spoken came about quickly and decidedly. The tree would no longer bear fruit, whether in season or out of season. If you read Matthew's account of the story, you'll see that it didn't even take the full day to take place: "Now in the morning, when He was returning to the city, He became hungry. Seeing a lone fig tree by the road, He came to it and found nothing on it except leaves only; and He said to it, 'No longer shall there ever be any fruit from you.' And at once the fig tree withered" (Matthew 21:18–19).

Both of the accounts are accurate. One person recorded the start of the process while the other recorded a more progressed state of being. When a tree dies, it dies at the root. You don't see the root. So while Christ's words took place immediately, the full manifestation took a day to play out. Whether in Matthew's account or in Mark's, Jesus' response to the disciples' astonishment was the same. He encouraged and reminded them to have faith in God. He wanted them to recognize what faith could produce. Faith is the access point into kingdom authority, which, as noted earlier, is the authorized right

Faith in God is the basis for the kingdom authority to change things and situations in your life.

to access divine power. Jesus never lacks faith. When He spoke to the tree to command that it wither, it withered. This is because His faith and confidence in what He said was enough to make it happen.

Of course it's easy to have faith when you *are* God. But Jesus was reminding His disciples that they, too, could have this level of faith. Faith in God is the basis for the kingdom authority to change things and situations in your life.

BREAKING BARRIERS OF FLAWED FAITH

Many people claim to have faith. And many of them probably do have faith. But in the story of the withered fig tree, Jesus made a point of saying to "have faith in God." The meaning of faith is tied to the object in which that faith is placed. To have faith in the Easter Bunny or the tooth fairy is to have faith in something that doesn't exist. Faith is only as meaningful and authoritative as the object (or person) you place that faith in. That means if you don't know God through His Son Jesus Christ, then you do not have an authoritative faith. Or if you have a wrong understanding of who God is, it can negatively affect your level of authoritative faith.

Some people even have faith in faith. They think that if they believe positive things or think positive thoughts long enough and hard enough, their faith in their own belief will produce what they want. But Jesus made a point of instructing His disciples that their faith needed to be placed in God. Not in a mantra. Not in a vibe. Not even in an affirmation.

It is God who has the kingdom authority to rule and overrule on earth. Unless the one true God is correctly in the picture of your belief system, your faith is empty. Flawed faith produces nothing. The object of your faith must be worthy of the trust for your faith to work.

Far too many Christians exercise a flawed faith either because they don't know God or because they have the wrong information about God. So they wind up expecting God to do something for them He never said He would do. As a result, they become disappointed in God. Jesus gave His disciples a clear example of what kingdom authority can produce. He wanted them to know that the same kingdom authority that He used to wither the fruitless fig tree was available to them. We know this because when the disciples asked how the fig tree withered, He followed up His answer with the following:

> "Truly I say to you, whoever says to this mountain, 'Be taken up and cast into the sea,' and does not doubt in his heart, but believes that what he says is going to happen, it will be granted him. Therefore I say to you, all things for which you pray and ask, believe that you have received them, and they will be granted you." (Mark 11:23–24)

Jesus quickly moved from a tree to a mountain to demonstrate the power of faith. He didn't want the disciples stuck on withering trees. He wanted to expand their view to include everything that had the potential to do with their faith.

In Scripture, a mountain was often symbolically used to illustrate a situation that was challenging or seemingly impossible to overcome (Zechariah 4:6–7; Matthew 17:20). It loomed large as a place where normal people couldn't climb. Mountains were also used by ruling powers and kingdoms. A mountain is anything that seeks to illegitimately control or defeat you. Mountains represented problems that had gotten too large or pain that had gotten too bad. Mountains could refer to finances having gotten too low, poor health, or anything outside of humanity's ability to fix itself. Jesus went straight for the thing the disciples knew they couldn't move or fix on their own. He wanted them to realize that what they were unable to fix due to the limitations of their own five senses and the finiteness of their humanity God could easily fix if they had faith in Him.

It's important to remember as you go through your life that to experience God's unleashing authority within you, you cannot rely on your own sense of touch, smell, hearing, taste, or sight as your guide. You must rely on God. Walking by faith means just that. It means you are willing to take steps out into the unknown because you know the One who knows all. Following God may seem risky, but it is not. It is the safest and most secure way to live out your days. If and when you become the source of your own confidence, you no longer have faith in God.

THE POWER OF GENUINE FAITH

As I've noted, mountains are those things that loom large before us that we cannot move in our own strength. If you could handle it on your own, it wouldn't be a mountain. If you could deal with it on your own, you wouldn't need faith. But if whatever it is you are facing consumes you and overwhelms you so that you do not know how to overcome it, Jesus has given us the faith techniques needed to unleash our spiritual victory: speaking to the issue at hand directly and speaking to God about the issue as well.

For starters, Jesus reminded us that we are to speak to the issues we face. This is important. The reason why this is important is because we have power in our words when coupled with faith. Far too many Christians waste the authority given to them in their words by using their words unwisely. When facing a mountain, they complain. When battling an issue, they grumble. When going through a trial or difficulty, they may blame or speak negatively. None of those things will enable you to overcome life's mountains. Jesus said that when you or I face a mountain, we are to speak to it in faith, without doubting. We read this in the context of Christ's reply to His disciples:

> Seeing this, the disciples were amazed and asked, "How did the fig tree wither all at once?" And Jesus answered and said to them, "Truly I say to you, if you have faith and do not doubt, you will not only do what was done to the fig tree, but even if you say to this mountain, 'Be taken up and cast into the sea,' it will happen. And all things you ask in prayer, believing, you will receive." (Matthew 21:20–22)

Jesus spoke to the fig tree when He said it would not bear any more fruit. He didn't speak about the fig tree. One of our primary problems and failures as believers in the body of Christ involves our tendency to speak about our problems, about our relationships, about our fears to others rather than to our mountains in faith. When you speak to your mountain, you introduce God and His character, power, and strength to whatever it is you are facing. You change your focus from the mountain itself to God. In speaking about your mountains or problems to others, you only magnify the size of the mountain and the problems. But in speaking to the mountain or problems about God and His power, you magnify God.

As you magnify God in your heart and mind, your faith grows. This enables you to speak to your mountain in faith, without doubting. God tells us to walk by faith. God is expecting you and me to do no less. And in this passage we discover that we are to also talk by faith. We are to speak to the mountains in our lives about God, His character, and His ability to overcome whatever we face. Proverbs 18:21 tells us, "Death and life are in the power of the tongue, and those who love it will eat its fruit."

To unleash God's power, peace, and provision in and through you, you must first grab hold of what is true about God, His character, and His Word. Then you must have a conversation with the mountain you face. That's why, even when Jesus had to deal with the devil in Matthew 4, He inserted God's Word into the conversation. Over and over we

When you speak to your mountain, you introduce God and His character, power, and strength to whatever it is you are facing.

read that Jesus responded to the devil with "It is written . . ." The truth of God is a powerful tool when used rightly. But it is difficult to use the Word of God rightly if you do not know the Word of God or spend enough time in the Word of God to familiarize yourself with God's character and values.

God has so set up our time on earth to offer us the opportunity of learning how to grow through difficulty. He allows the chaos, confusion, and challenges because He turned the earth over to humanity long ago. We see this in Psalm 115:16: "The heavens are the heavens of the Lord, but the earth He has given to the sons of men." The heavens and heavenly realm belong to God.

And while the earth also belongs to Him ultimately, for this period of time—this dispensation—He has turned over the managerial rule of earth to humanity. He has placed us here with the dominion to rule. Whether we rule and make decisions that are good or bad is up to us. But we must remember that the consequences of those decisions are baked in. When we manage poorly, chaos ensues. When we honor God and rule according to His kingdom principles, the values of the kingdom are made manifest.

Thus, if you choose not to include God in your decision-making or choices, or even in seeking to overcome obstacles in your life, He will respect your choice not to include Him. But He will also allow you to face the repercussions built into not including Him. Like with Adam and Eve in the garden, if you choose to eat from the forbidden tree, you will be making the choice to leave the garden.

It's easy to blame God when difficulties come into our

lives, but what we often forget is that our own choices led to those difficulties. God will never force our obedience, but He does reward it. One of the ways He rewards obedience and faith is through unleashing His supernatural power that He delegates to us when we call on Him to do so.

If you say to the mountain that it should be removed, and if you say it without doubting in your heart—it will be removed. Not only that, if you turn to God and direct your conversation to Him after speaking directly to your mountain about Him, He will respond to you. Let's revisit Mark 11:24: "Therefore I say to you, all things for which you pray and ask, believe that you have received them, and they will be granted you."

You are to do two things, in any order, when facing a difficulty. One of them is to have a conversation with the mountain itself. The second thing you are to do is to talk to God about the mountain. Here's another way to think of it: Talk to the problem about God; talk to God about the problem. Unfortunately, far too many of us do neither. Instead, we talk to other people about the problem. Then we talk to ourselves about the problem again. If you've done that enough times, you should know by now it doesn't work. Not only does it fail to move mountains, but it usually even makes the mountains grow.

Jesus emphasized through this experience with His disciples that faith needs to be futuristic while simultaneously past tense. Now, before you scratch your head, let me explain. When Jesus said to speak to the mountain, He said that if you tell the mountain to be cast into the sea, believing it will happen, it will take place (Mark 11:23). That's futuristic faith. You are believing that something is going to happen.

But Jesus also said that when you pray to God in faith, you are to pray and believe you have received your answer (Mark 11:24). That's past-tense faith. You believe what you asked for has already taken place. Let's look at these two verses more closely:

> **Futuristic Faith:** "Truly I say to you, whoever says to this mountain, 'Be taken up and cast into the sea,' and does not doubt in his heart, but believes that what he says is going to happen, it will be granted him" (v. 23).

> **Past-Tense Faith:** "Therefore I say to you, all things for which you pray and ask, believe that you have received them, and they will be granted you" (v. 24).

In the span of two short verses we are given two very different ways to pray. We are shown two different perspectives on how to have faith. What's more, they aren't mutually exclusive. We are to do both of these in conjunction with each other. While you are believing God will do what you are praying for in faith, you are also to believe that He has already done it. See, God is not bound by time or space. What He has determined to do has already been decided because He is not limited by a past or a future. His perspective in heaven differs from our reality on earth because He sees all and knows all. While you and I experience a gap between when we pray and when our prayers are answered,

God knows no bounds. He doesn't have to sit and guess whether something is going to come about, because He's been to the future and back again. He embodies all time within Him. That's important to remember as you pray. You are not only having faith that something will happen; you are having faith that it has already happened.

BRIDGING HEAVEN AND EARTH

Faith creates a bridge between what God has already declared and what you are going to see manifested. In our existence, there is a time gap between the spiritual root and the physical fruit. Something may have been decided and declared in heaven, yet it takes time for it to be revealed on earth. Going back to one of my favorite illustrations—electricity—will help me illustrate this point.

Faith creates a bridge between what God has already declared and what you are going to see manifested.

You and I both have electricity in our homes. We have a power connection from our home to a local power provider. If you pay your bills on time, that power flows continuously to your home. But just because you and I have power doesn't mean we will benefit from it. Like we discussed earlier, the only way to benefit from the power running to a home is through plugging in whatever device or item needs the power. The electric company is not going to send someone to your home to plug in your devices, lightbulbs, refrigerator, or any other needed item for you. If you want to use the power, you have to connect to the power source through a plug.

What God has set up for us in His conditional will is that when the qualifications He has established have been met, the answer to the request will be revealed. God's primary qualifications revolve around faith and belief in Him. They also include aligning under His rule and abiding with Him as John 15 states: "If you abide in Me, and My words abide in you, ask whatever you wish, and it will be done for you" (v. 7). Prayer is not like placing an Amazon order. We must be relationally connected to God.

A lot of us have answers to our prayers still hanging out in heaven because they have never been drawn down to earth, simply due to the qualifications not being met. God functions with both a conditional and unconditional will. His unconditional will involves those things He is going to do regardless of what anyone else says or does. But He also has a conditional will. That means He will only do it if the conditions have been met. We see this in 1 John 5:14–15: "This is the confidence which we have before Him, that, if we ask anything according to His will, He hears us. And if we know that He hears us in whatever we ask, we know that we have the requests which we have asked from Him."

In this passage we see one clear condition for answered prayer: asking according to God's will. When you pray according to God's will, He will answer according to your prayer. That's why discerning the will of God through an abiding relationship with the Holy Spirit is so important. When you pray according to God's will, your answers no longer get stuck in the ionosphere, never to manifest in your life on earth. God desires to answer your prayers and unleash His authority both in you and through you. But He has set up certain conditions to bring this about. God has so established the world as a free-will environment that He is often dependent upon what we each decide to do through our own choices and beliefs.

Another story in Scripture illustrates this principle perfectly. We read about it in Matthew 17:

> When they came to the crowd, a man came up to Jesus, falling on his knees before Him and saying, "Lord, have mercy on my son, for he is a lunatic and is very ill; for he often falls into the fire and often into the water. I brought him to Your disciples, and they could not cure him." And Jesus answered and said, "You unbelieving and perverted generation, how long shall I be with you? How long shall I put up with you? Bring him here to Me." And Jesus rebuked him, and the demon came out of him, and the boy was cured at once.
>
> Then the disciples came to Jesus privately and said, "Why could we not drive it out?" And He said to them, "Because of the littleness of your faith; for truly I say to you, if you have faith the size of a mustard seed, you will say to this mountain, 'Move from here to there,' and it will move; and nothing will be impossible to you." (vv. 14–20)

This is often referred to as the story of the demoniac. It revolves around a father and a son. The son struggles with a mental illness and is plagued by a demon, so the father brings him to Jesus and asks for His help. The interesting part is that the father had already brought his son to the disciples, but they were unable to help. What's more, when Jesus heard about that, He got what I like to call "evangelically ticked off!" That's not an exaggeration. His words underscore His frustration: "You unbelieving and perverted generation, how long shall I be with you? How long shall I put up with you?" Jesus was upset at the unbelief in those around Him. Their lack of belief meant the problem did not get resolved. Their lack of faith contributed to the ongoing pain of the demoniac, who would throw himself into the fire, and the ongoing pain of his father.

All Jesus had to do was rebuke the demon and he came out. All it took was belief tied to the authority of Jesus for the boy to be cured immediately. I'm sure the disciples were not only shocked but also embarrassed. We can see that because they later went to talk with Him "privately." They asked Jesus why they couldn't do what He had just done. To which He replied, "Because of the littleness of your faith." The reason why the disciples couldn't produce change in the lives of others was due to their flawed belief system. Jesus was so frustrated with them that He told them they needed faith the size of a mustard seed. That could have been like adding insult to injury. A mustard seed is infinitesimally small. Yet even in the disciples' "littleness" of faith, it wasn't as big as a mustard seed. The disciples' problem, and ours, is that they had a small view of God. A little faith in a big God can work miracles.

Jesus knew their faith was tarnished by doubt. He could see this in their actions. Anytime your faith comes mixed with doubt, your actions will reveal it. That is because if you truly believe something has happened, you won't still be trying to make it happen. Or you won't still be worrying that it won't happen. Praying with a past-tense form of faith—knowing God has already purposed to do it—shows up in your actions. For example, you wouldn't go to an online shopping app and order the same thing every day simply because the first time you ordered it, it took a few days to be delivered. Rather, you would order it once and go on about your life, knowing it will arrive when the seller said it would.

Faith never forces God's hand. Faith simply accesses what God has already planned.

Faith never forces God's hand. Faith simply accesses what God has already planned. It doesn't make Him do something He never intended to. None of us can make God do anything other than what is in His will. But what we can do is access, even unleash, His manifest will in our lives. Living in God's will is far better than struggling to make it on your own.

Understanding what it takes to tap into His power and might starts by increasing and expanding your faith. Increase your faith to that of a mustard seed or more, and then watch what God will do. Expand your faith to include not only the future but also the past tense, and you'll be amazed. Unfortunately many people get disappointed with God, when, in fact, God is disappointed with them. He has the answers to all we need, but He has given us conditions as to how those answers will be obtained.

REMOVING FAITH OBSTACLES THROUGH FORGIVENESS

Jesus also gives another, often unnoticed, condition, along with faith and prayer, for us to be able to unleash authority over our mountains. He said unforgiveness will stifle God's work in our lives (Mark 11:25–26).

The story is told of an elderly couple who went to the doctor because the husband thought his wife was hard of hearing. The husband explained to the doctor that she didn't seem to hear anything at all. The doctor asked for an example, so the husband shared how the previous night in the kitchen, he asked his wife what she was cooking. He waited, but there was no answer. So he decided to move closer, roughly ten feet away, and asked again. Still no answer. Finally he moved right beside her, but still he did not get an answer.

When the doctor turned to the wife to ask whether she had heard him, she replied, "Yes, of course I heard him—I answered him three times!"

In other words, sometimes the problem isn't the problem. Or the problem isn't God turning a deaf ear. Or the problem isn't the mountain itself. The problem just may be your needing to increase and expand your faith in God and then speak it out loud.

Chapter Three

CHASING LIFE'S ESSENTIALS

Kingdom Pursuit

ONE OF THE MAJOR ISSUES WE WRESTLE WITH IN AMERICA involves our borders. Some people have labeled this a "border crisis." It involves an influx of individuals seeking residence in this "kingdom" called the United States because they feel their lives would be much improved if they came here. At great personal risk, while also leaving what they know and, often, who they know behind, they press hard to get to a place they feel will be a step up for them.

But then we also have people who live in the United States who were born here. These are citizens of this "kingdom" called the United States. Unfortunately, some of these citizens seek to illegitimately take advantage of the benefits this nation has to offer.

Thus, we have two groups of people who are trying to access the benefits of this nation inappropriately. Some don't belong here but seek the benefits of living here. Others do belong here but seek to dishonestly or unethically take advantage of the benefits our country provides. Both groups have flaws.

Similarly, in God's world there are many who are not a legitimate part of His covenantal kingdom through faith alone in the shed blood of Jesus Christ, but they still seek to access the benefits of the kingdom. They don't want to align their lives under the rule of Jesus, but they do want the favor and blessing of God. Then there are also those who are saved by faith in Jesus but who choose not to live a life according to His will. Yet, even so, they attempt to illegitimately take advantage of the benefits of God's kingdom. Or they complain and blame when they do not experience the benefits and favor God has prepared for those in His kingdom who follow Him.

As a reminder, *the* kingdom of God refers to the governmental realm of His rule. When we go to the original term tied to "kingdom," which is *basileia*, it references the rule or authority of a realm. It was a common term to indicate ruling bodies in localized regions of people, cities, or cultures. Thus, God's kingdom is His sphere of rule. So important is this subject that it is the central theme of Scripture. The Bible's theme is the glory of God through the advancement of His kingdom. I refer to this advancement as God's kingdom agenda.

I've defined it before but let's rehearse it again for our time together in this chapter. The kingdom agenda is the visible manifestation of the comprehensive rule of God over every area of life. God wants His rule to affect and influence all of life. When that is accomplished, He gets the glory. People who align themselves beneath God's kingdom agenda by promoting God's glory according to His principles of rule are entitled to His benefits. However, far too many people today seek to usurp God's rule in their lives and simultaneously remove themselves from the reach of His favor.

Then there are also those who are not Christians at all. They are not in His kingdom. When these individuals try to tap into God's benefits and favor, they lack the spiritual authority to do so. Oftentimes they may even attend church or be fervent in "religion," but without an abiding, saving relationship with Jesus, they are unable to gain access to the kingdom of God and the benefits that come from it.

NATURE'S LESSON ON TRUSTING GOD

Only those who know Christ as their Savior and live with Christ as their Lord can fully unleash God's kingdom blessings. In Luke 12, Jesus explained this in detail. He spoke about how to maximize the benefits of the kingdom as His follower:

> He said to His disciples, "For this reason I say to you, do not worry about your life, as to what you will eat; nor for your body, as to what you will put on. For life is more than food, and the body more than clothing. Consider the ravens, for they neither sow nor reap; they have no storeroom nor barn, and yet God feeds them; how much more valuable you are than the birds! And which of you by worrying can add a single hour to his life's span? If then you cannot do even a very little thing, why do you worry about other matters? Consider the lilies, how they grow: they neither toil nor spin; but I tell you, not even Solomon in all his glory clothed himself like one of these. But if God so clothes the grass in the field, which is alive today and tomorrow is thrown into the furnace, how much more will He clothe you? You men of little faith! And do not seek what you will eat and what you will drink, and do not keep worrying. For all these things the nations of the world eagerly seek; but your Father knows that you need these things." (vv. 22–30)

Jesus offered an elaborate illustration based on nature to explain how abiding under God's rule in the kingdom allows for a life of peace, rest, and provision. God clothes the grass. God creates the lilies. God feeds the birds. And He does all of this without them having to beg, fret, borrow, or steal.

What Jesus wanted His disciples to hear from this portrait of God's provision is that God will also give them all they need when they first recognize Him. We see this emphasis in verses 31–32: "But seek His kingdom, and these things will be added to you. Do not be afraid, little flock, for your Father has chosen gladly to give you the kingdom."

We are to "seek" God's kingdom. The number one priority for every believer is to seek God's kingdom. We read this again in Matthew 6:33: "But seek first His kingdom and His righteousness, and all these things will be added to you." The word *seek* means to pursue something as a passionate priority. It means to actively and intentionally place God and His rule as first in your life.

See, there are a few things God cannot do. I know we like to say that God can do anything, but that's not quite true. There are some things God cannot do. One of these is found in Hebrews 6:18: "So that by two unchangeable things in which it is impossible for God to lie, we who have taken refuge would have strong encouragement to take hold of the hope set before us." God cannot lie.

Another thing God cannot do is be second. He will not accept a second-place prioritization in your life. Anytime someone or something gets more of your focus, attention, or prioritization than God, that someone or something has become an idol. Anytime God is not first, He is eclipsed by an idol. He will not tolerate that. Just like a run doesn't count if a baseball player fails to step on first base before proceeding to round the bases to home plate, the promises of God's kingdom and His covenantal blessings do not flow to you when you fail to put Him first. All of these blessings and the unleashing of His spiritual authority go out the window when you choose not to place the rule and jurisdiction of God as first place in your life.

God wants you to pursue His reign and His rule. He wants you to pursue His agenda. He wants you to apply His thinking, His principles, and His approach to every area of your life. Until you do that, you won't be unleashing much of anything good at all. God is not to be used like a spare tire—there if you need it in a desperate situation but ignored and forgotten at all other times. Unfortunately, what many people do is seek God when life goes flat or they hit a bump, but they keep Him in the trunk until the next flat occurs.

God has made it clear that we ought to seek His kingdom first, at all times. Above all else. This is not a pie-in-the-sky concept. This is not a suggestion. Seeking and pursuing God and His kingdom first is what unleashes the work of His kingdom in your life. Bringing God's perspective from heaven into history unveils His will on earth. We are not to allow the kingdom of this culture to cause us to miss the kingdom of God and His agenda. Rather, we must make a big deal of prioritizing God in our decision-making. When you do that, you will receive spiritual benefits—one of them being a reduction in stress and worry.

Seeking and pursuing God and His kingdom first is what unleashes the work of His kingdom in your life.

BE SET FREE FROM WORRY

We live in a day when worry, anxiety, and stress are at an all-time high. More people are medicated for anxiety now than ever before.[1] Stress affects not only our relationships and outlook but also our health. Much of what we suffer from physically has its root in stress and stress hormones.

But there is a simple solution to overcoming worry, anxiety, and stress. That solution involves seeking God and His kingdom first in your life. We can see this when we look at the context within which Jesus instructed His disciples to seek the kingdom. We already looked at Luke 12:22–30, where He told them to do that. But the verses leading up to that statement are just as revealing. Jesus was in the midst of talking to them about this area of worry when He gave them this important life truth:

> "I say to you, My friends, do not be afraid of those who kill the body and after that have no more that they can do." (v. 4)

> "Indeed, the very hairs of your head are all numbered. Do not fear; you are more valuable than many sparrows." (v. 7)

> "When they bring you before the synagogues and the rulers and the authorities, do not worry about how or what you are to speak in your defense, or what you are to say; for the Holy Spirit will teach you in that very hour what you ought to say." (vv. 11–12)

> And He said to His disciples, "For this reason I say to you, do not worry about your life, as to what you will eat; nor for your body, as to what you will put on." (v. 22)

> "And which of you by worrying can add a single hour to his life's span? If then you cannot do even a very little thing, why do you worry about other matters?" (vv. 25–26)

> "And do not seek what you will eat and what you will drink, and do not keep worrying. For all these things the nations of the world eagerly seek; but your Father knows that you need these things." (vv. 29–30)

> "Do not be afraid, little flock, for your Father has chosen gladly to give you the kingdom." (v. 32)

Jesus instructed the disciples to seek God's kingdom first in the context of telling them they did not need to worry or be afraid. The entire passage centers on this theme. That tells us that one of the premier benefits of seeking God and His kingdom involves a freedom from worry, stress, and fear. God has given us the formula for living a peace-filled, calm life based on confidence in Him. He's given us the prescription for peace and the antidote to anxiety. We can live a life of peace when we prioritize Christ.

Keep in mind, He wasn't talking about concerns that require our attention to address them. There are many things in life that can be concerning and need us to focus on them at that time. But worry is concern gone haywire. For example, you can control your concern. But worry controls you. Worry is where concern has become a monster in your mind. Worry tells you when you can sleep and when you can't. Worry tells you when you can have fun and when you can't. Worry dictates what you do, think, and say. If you want to unleash the power to overcome worry in your life, it begins with seeking the kingdom of God first.

The story is told about a man who was worried about a great number of things. He considered that if anything else went wrong, it would take him two weeks to get to the point where he was free to worry about it. He already had too many things to worry about. That's when he decided to see if he could pay someone else to worry for him. Someone answered his ad to worry for him for $1,000. The person asked when he would get paid. But the man replied, "Well, that's the first thing you need to worry about!"

If you want to unleash the power to overcome worry in your life, it begins with seeking the kingdom of God first.

It's a humorous story but has an underlying truth. We are often so consumed with pain, fear, and difficulties that we don't even know where we can find the time or strength to worry about something new or something else. Jesus commands us not to worry. In fact, He says we are to stop it. We are to stop letting our concerns control us as worry. Worry is like a rocking chair or a treadmill. It gets you started and keeps you busy, but it doesn't take you anywhere.

Jesus puts our worry into perspective when He reminds us to prioritize God. When He told us we are not to worry about what we eat, it was a reminder that the greater worry would be whether we wake up the next day and have the opportunity to eat. Once we recognize that God Himself holds our entire life in His hands, it puts our daily concerns in perspective. We ought to prioritize God because God is the ultimate ruler over all. We shouldn't worry about what we wear, because it is God who determines whether we even have the strength to get up and get dressed at all. Perspective matters. Once we realign our thinking from the world's viewpoint to God's viewpoint, we can quickly identify what matters most.

The worries and anxieties that we frequently prioritize with our time, energy, and conversations are typically what I call secondary concerns. How many of us worry whether there is enough oxygen available today to breathe? How many of us worry whether our heart will keep beating today? How many of us worry whether our joints will work today? Probably only those who are deficient or struggling in any of those areas. We often take God's provision for granted and fixate on secondary concerns as if they were the greatest concerns to have. God is our source, provider, and supplier of all we need. When you and I prioritize our pursuit of Him, we discover that He is able to take care of not only our primary concerns but our secondary ones as well.

An acorn is an oak waiting to happen. An acorn doesn't worry whether it will become an oak. Neither does it strategize. An acorn rests in the reality that all it needs to become an oak is built in. Plants, fruits, and vegetables have seeds built into them that allow them to replicate and to continue to live. God has so designed our world that we have within us what we need to go on. He's looked over every detail from the bears to the birds, providing food, nourishment, water, and an environment conducive to how each is designed. If God has provided so well for nature and the wildlife, why do we so often think He will forget about us? I don't know about you, but since He is my provider and sustainer, I want to prioritize my relationship with Him.

Some people need an oxygen tank to help deliver needed air to their lungs for every breath. Do you think they prioritize their relationship with their oxygen tank? Would they be concerned with where their oxygen tank was and whether it was in close proximity to them? Would they want to be sure the oxygen tank had all it needed to function, whether that involved electricity or other working parts? When we realize our dependency on an inanimate object for our very life itself, we will prioritize that inanimate object. Yet so many of us have forgotten how deeply dependent we are on God. We have forgotten that He is our source of life itself. When we realize this, we will make the pursuit of Him the first priority in all we do.

When it comes to worry, your number one priority should be to stop it. When worrying thoughts creep up, stop them. One way to stop worrying is to shift your focus and confidence to the goodness of God. Philippians 4:6–9 reiterates this approach:

> Be anxious for nothing, but in everything by prayer and supplication with thanksgiving let your requests be made

> known to God. And the peace of God, which surpasses all comprehension, will guard your hearts and your minds in Christ Jesus.
>
> Finally, brethren, whatever is true, whatever is honorable, whatever is right, whatever is pure, whatever is lovely, whatever is of good repute, if there is any excellence and if anything worthy of praise, dwell on these things. The things you have learned and received and heard and seen in me, practice these things, and the God of peace will be with you.

This passage provides the way for each of us to live a worry-free life. First, we are to pray with a heart of gratitude, being thankful that God is our source and we are not victims of a chaotic world, as it may seem. Then we are to shift our thoughts onto whatever is true, honorable, pure, and lovely, and concepts that are of good repute. We are to think about that which is excellent and praiseworthy—first and foremost being God. As we do these things—pray and align our thoughts under God's perspective—we will stop worrying.

THE POWER OF PRIORITIZING GOD

The problem too many people face is a lack of seeing God as their provider, their caregiver, and even their Father. Jesus intentionally used the term *Father* when speaking on seeking God and His kingdom. As a refresher, He said: "For all these things the nations of the world eagerly seek; but your Father knows that you need these things. But seek His kingdom, and these things will be added to you" (Luke 12:30–31).

Not everyone has had a good experience with their earthly fathers, so this concept of a good Father may be distant. But when Jesus spoke these words, helping us to identify God as a caring Father, He was referring to the positive and excellent qualities in a father. And while God is supremely God—omnipotent, omniscient, and omnipresent—He is also Daddy. He is also a relational God who desires to be close to you and me. He has all the attributes of a good father: kindness, love, care, provision, empathy, and more. A good father pursues the well-being and development of his child, providing all that is needed to launch his child into adulthood successfully. A good father would never leave his children in a situation where they would be left to fend for themselves. He would not abandon his children in need. Good fathers will often do this even at great personal sacrifice. God, as our good Father, does this as well. And more.

This principle of God's unleashing His presence and provision is so simple but often overlooked. Pursuing God as the priority in our life is the principle. It should be the guiding principle in all we do. Instead of making decisions that support our goals and agenda, make decisions that support God's kingdom agenda. Once we learn to reorient ourselves to prioritizing God over self, culture, and relationships, we will unleash God's power in our life.

If you choose to abandon God's kingdom program in order to allow the culture, secular society, your friends, or even your own thoughts and desires to become your priority, you cannot expect God's favor. You cannot expect God's power. You cannot expect God's divine provision. Just like a good father would not enable his children to continue in drug abuse or supply his children's addictive habits either financially or with the substance itself, God will not enable you in your pursuit of anything other than Him. He will allow you to live a life earmarked by idolatry. That's what free will is. But He will not supernaturally supply you with all you need if you are making other things an idol over Him.

God desires to give you peace, calm, provision, and all that you need. But He has made it clear what is required of you in order to access these things. He requires your obedience, your alignment, and your seeking His kingdom above all.

I'll never forget when I was in seminary and barely making enough of an income while working part-time to support my family. Things had gotten so tight financially that I talked with Lois about dropping out of seminary. We had three small kids at the time, and the money just wasn't stretching far enough to cover our bills.

Lois and I decided to pray and ask God for His provision. We needed $500 to make it through the end of the month. If we didn't get $500 in the next few days, I would need to drop out and get a job that would make an extra $500 quickly. In fact, I told Lois that if we didn't get the $500 by the end of the day, I would drop out of seminary and get a full-time job until I was able to go back to seminary, possibly the next semester.

If you choose to abandon God's kingdom program in order to allow the culture, secular society, your friends, or even your own thoughts and desires to become your priority, you cannot expect God's favor.

When I went to class that day, I stopped by the campus mailboxes to pick up my mail. When I opened the mailbox, I pulled out an envelope with five crisp $100 bills in it. There was no name or note. It wasn't until years later that the person who had given me the money told me that God had put it on his heart to give me exactly $500 that day. That gift kept me in seminary. The Holy Spirit provided by inspiring someone to meet our family's need at a critical time.

It's God's good pleasure to give us the kingdom when we pursue Him first. Putting God first means living according to His values. I knew, as a father and a husband, that God's values were to care for the needs of my family first. If I could not do that and attend seminary at the same time, then I knew which one I had to relinquish. When God saw that I was willing to relinquish my pursuit of a degree so that I could take care of the needs of my family, He stepped in and supplied. Seeking God's kingdom first is the key to unleashing God's kingdom in your life.

Chapter Four

A LIFE THAT STANDS FIRM

Kingdom Commitment

IF YOU WERE TO ATTEND COLLEGE AND AUDIT A COURSE, what you are indicating is that you want the information but none of the responsibility. Auditing often entails having a learner listen to what the teacher has to say but not participate in any of the course papers or tests. Auditing is information gathering without the willingness to demonstrate how much of that information you retained.

Many people come to church in a similar fashion. They want the information. They want the music. They want to greet their friends or show off their latest outfit. But they don't want to take part in any of the responsibilities. In fact, most people merely audit church. Not only that, but most people merely audit the Christian faith. These are what we call cultural Christians. They attach Christianity to their environment, vocabulary, or routines as part of a cultural nuance. Since Christianity was a dominant religion in America for many years, many people chose to become cultural Christians simply to fit in or find a benefit for themselves.

But cultural Christians don't allow their faith to affect them at the identity level. It's more of a label than an authentic expression of true faith. Cultural Christians toss in a prayer here and there, show up at church from time to time, and have a Bible app on their phones for a verse a day to keep the devil away. Beyond that, there isn't much depth.

Not only do we have a number of cultural Christians today, but we also have what I call casual Christians. Casual Christians are involved in their faith more than cultural Christians, but it's as if they use it conveniently. Christianity is seen to them as a crutch to lean on when needed. Some people might call casual Christians convenient Christians. These individuals make appearances at every holiday and special event. They apply some of the principles of Scripture—that which is convenient to them and may benefit them. But many of those in this category are not Christians at all. They are Christians by association, not by relationship.

Then there are also those who are truly saved, born-again believers. But they have not yet graduated to become a true disciple of Jesus Christ. The reason they haven't graduated is that they do not want the responsibility or obligation of discipleship. They just want to make sure that heaven is their home without any expectation of personal spiritual responsibility during their time on earth.

THE COST OF DISCIPLESHIP

Jesus knows each of these groups well. That's why, when He spoke about discipleship in Luke 9, He described each group separately. He wanted us to see the distinctions of discipleship levels. We gain a glimpse into this in verses 57–62:

> As they were going along the road, someone said to Him, "I will follow You wherever You go." And Jesus said to him, "The foxes have holes and the birds of the air have nests, but the Son of Man has nowhere to lay His head." And He said to another, "Follow Me." But he said, "Lord, permit me first to go and bury my father." But He said to him, "Allow the dead to bury their own dead; but as for you, go and proclaim everywhere the kingdom of God." Another also said, "I will follow You, Lord; but first permit me to say good-bye to those at home." But Jesus said to him, "No one, after putting his hand to the plow and looking back, is fit for the kingdom of God."

You have been called to follow Jesus; Jesus has not been called to follow you. Too many people make Christianity about Jesus following them.

In each of these three scenarios, the word *follow* appears. This is important to point out because the foundation of our spiritual life rests on following Jesus. Later in Luke, Jesus connected following Him to the kingdom with the jurisdiction of God's rule. You have been called to follow Jesus; Jesus has not been called to follow you. Too many people make Christianity about Jesus following them. They want Jesus to bless their plans, ideas, and desires. But kingdom living involves following Jesus. The root of discipleship is a commitment to following Christ (Luke 9:23, 57–62; 14:25–27; 18:22).

Let's look at this more closely through Jesus' illustration of the three people He told to follow Him.

Following Jesus in the Good Times and the Bad

The first person seemed very eager to follow the Lord. In fact, he said, "I will follow You wherever You go" (Luke 9:57). But Jesus knew his heart. He knew that was just him talking. He knew this man desired comfort, so He told him there may not be a place to sleep. In other words, He told him they may be roughing it instead of staying at the Ritz.

When Matthew told the same story, he gave us more information on the person speaking. While Luke didn't identify the man, Matthew let us know it was a scribe who spoke to Jesus. We read in Matthew 8:19: "Then a scribe came and said to Him, 'Teacher, I will follow You wherever You go.'" A scribe was a scholar in biblical days. Scribes loved learning. They loved Bible study. They loved getting into the nooks and crannies of bibliocentric, exegetical, expositional nuances and divinely ordained truth. Scribes wanted to pick the law apart in all of its idiosyncratic distinctions. That's why we shouldn't be surprised when this scribe referred to Jesus as "Teacher." He thought he had found a great teacher, and he wanted to sit at His feet to learn from Him.

The verses preceding this story give us insight into Jesus' popularity at that time. He was performing many miracles. People loved Him. No doubt this scribe saw the crowds grow around Jesus, and so he wanted to be a part of the new hit single on the streets. He wanted to hang out with Jesus, studying and learning from the best of the best. But Jesus knew his heart. Jesus knew what this man wanted. Jesus knew he wasn't a true follower or disciple. Jesus knew this man's ability to follow Him came with conditions—the first of which was a nice place to sleep. That's why Jesus let him know that if he came with Him, it would be hit-and-miss on where they would sleep. He wanted the scribe to know up front that this wasn't a retreat at the Four Seasons. In fact, they may even be homeless from time to time.

Jesus wanted to see if the man was in it for the stuff or for Him. He wanted to know whether the man was a prosperity-theology advocate or truly a kingdom disciple. Don't get me wrong. God is not opposed to prospering His people. He's not against improving your life through your work, diligence, or investments. But it's not all about that. The problem with prosperity theology is that it leaves out the doctrine of suffering. God does bless people, as we see in the life of Job. But God also allows people to suffer loss or go without—as we also see in the life of Job. Too many people assume that when things go left in their lives, God went left. They think that when the money gets funny, God let them down. Or if they get sick, that God is punishing them. But God works through both the good and the bad to bring about good for those who love Him and are called according to His purpose (Romans 8:28).

What Jesus wanted to know about this scribe was whether he would follow Him in the good times and the bad. He wanted to know if the man would bail out on a rough day. Jesus knew there were rough days ahead. He knew it would not always be like it was right then. His popularity would soon crash to the point of Him being hung on a cross. So He asked the man how deep his commitment truly was. We don't get to see the man's reply in the book of Luke, but we can assume that he, like the Pharisees when Jesus wrote in the sand while kneeling by the adulterous woman, simply slipped away.

The question Jesus posed to this scribe is a question for all of us as well. Are you following Jesus because of your love for Jesus or do you come to church and read your Bible for the kingdom goodies He offers? Sure, there are benefits to following Jesus, but Jesus wants to be sure that we are also game for the difficulties. God is not looking for gold diggers. Gold diggers want to attach themselves to others not because

**Are you following Jesus
because of your love for Jesus
or do you come to church
and read your Bible for the
kingdom goodies He offers?**

they love them but because they get stuff from them. A lot of people will hang out with God for His goodies. They will praise God in hopes of His provision. But when things go south, they simply slip away. They do not proclaim, like Job: "Though He slay me, I will hope in Him. Nevertheless I will argue my ways before Him" (Job 13:15).

I've shared this before but it's a good example. When I first started traveling and speaking and our kids were young, I would bring them back a gift. It was usually something small I picked up at the airport. After a while, the kids started asking me when I was going on my next trip. In other words, they no longer missed me. They just wanted what I could give them, what they could get from me.

A lot of people want Jesus for what they can get. But Jesus wants to know if you are following Him out of love for Him and a commitment to Him. That is the mark of a true follower of Christ. The first man in the story—the scribe—just wanted to hang out with the popular social influencer of the day: Jesus Christ. The scribe had no intention of following Jesus through thick and thin. Jesus knew that about him and called him out on it.

Letting Go of Security for the Kingdom

The next person who wanted to follow Jesus was also hesitant to do so when it came to surrendering all to follow Jesus. We see this by his response when Jesus told him to follow Him. The man replied, "Lord, permit me first to go and bury my father." At first glance, his request seems reasonable. In fact, it could even seem noble. The man was so committed to his family of origin that he simply wanted to do the right thing. But Jesus' response demonstrates otherwise.

Jesus' response surely caught the man off guard, as it may some of us reading this passage now. Jesus told him to let the dead bury the dead. We read, "But He said to him, 'Allow the dead to bury their own dead; but as for you, go and proclaim everywhere the kingdom of God'" (Luke 9:60). Keep in mind, the second man heard the conversation Jesus had with the scribe. He had insight that following Jesus may involve some difficult days ahead. He had come to the understanding that things might be financially tight if he were to follow the Lord. So he suggested that once he gets his inheritance from his father, he could follow Jesus. That way, if Jesus didn't know where He would sleep at night, at least this man would have a nice warm hotel room. This man wanted to get his security system set in place first. He wanted to have his retirement in order. But Jesus saw through it all.

Jesus let this man know that the spiritually dead must bury the spiritually dead. I can say this because dead people can't bury dead people. So when Jesus said to let the dead bury the dead, He was referring to the spiritually dead (that is, unbelievers). We are never to let our desire for security interfere with our spiritual purpose. To put it another way, Jesus was saying that we are not to allow our physical or personal desires for security to keep us from fulfilling our spiritual priorities.

In the New Testament culture, when a person was buried, they were buried quickly because they did not have the embalming process we have today. In addition to that, if a

Jewish person was next to a dead body, then that person would be considered unclean for a week. Those two things alone let us know that this man was not talking about a physical reality. He was not in a hurry to go bury his father right then. Rather, he was remarking that when his father eventually passed away, he would follow Jesus. He wanted to get his physical and financial priorities shored up before making a spiritual commitment. Dotting the i's and crossing the t's should never come before following Jesus Christ. Following Jesus comes with faith. When Jesus asks you to follow Him, He's asking you to follow Him now.

Following Jesus comes with faith. When Jesus asks you to follow Him, He's asking you to follow Him now.

Jesus knew that in order for the second man to follow Him, he had to have his priorities straight or he would bail out when things got hard. This second man reminds me of the story of a farmer who put an ad for a wife in the paper: "Looking for a marriage-minded woman with a tractor. I've got a hundred acres of land. Send me a picture of the tractor." It's a humorous story but it reflects the conditional commitment so many people have. They will follow Jesus as long as they get what they want. Jesus' point is that the kingdom can't wait, so stop postponing discipleship.

Breaking Free from a Divided Mind

Finally, let's look at the third person Jesus spoke to in the conversation recorded in Luke 9. This individual had heard the first two conversations. He knew what was in store. He wanted to make a good first impression on Jesus, so he made his condition much lighter in nature. He said, "I will follow You, Lord; but first permit me to say good-bye to those at home" (v. 61). He didn't think he was asking for much. He just wanted a quick goodbye to his family. Surely that was okay. But Jesus knew his heart. He knew his commitment wasn't nearly as strong as he had insinuated through his words.

Jesus knew this was a rearview-mirror kind of follower. He was okay with moving forward as long as he could keep looking back. That's why Jesus told him that no one who puts his hand to the plow is fit for the kingdom if he looks back. You can't have both. Anyone who plows while glancing backward is going to wind up with a curved line. It's like the Israelites when they left Egypt. They were in the desert and wanted to go back to Egypt because they were comparing their present-day reality with their past. This led to grumbling, complaining, and resentment. Jesus didn't want a resentful follower always saying, "Well, this is how we did it where I come from." That mindset creates a jaded focus. Jesus wasn't recruiting consultants. He wanted kingdom followers who were committed to the kingdom of God.

What's more, in biblical culture, goodbyes could last for weeks. Many of the houseguests in that day and age stayed around for months at a time. There wasn't the tradition of walking someone to their car, patting them on the back, and seeing them off. A goodbye was a long, drawn-out experience. Jesus knew the man wasn't asking for an opportunity to say goodbye that afternoon. Rather, he wanted to go hang out with his homies and draw it out as long as possible. He wanted to eat his favorite dishes. He wanted to watch his favorite shows. He wanted to converse with his favorite people. The man, essentially, wanted both, resulting in indecisiveness. He wanted to follow Jesus while also maintaining a strong connection to his home. But Jesus wouldn't stand for that. Jesus wants committed disciples who will not look back to what was left behind.

We are not to postpone our commitment for a more convenient time. We are not to hold out for a better offer. We are not to wait until we have our retirement in place. Jesus asks us to follow Him when He says to follow Him because advancing the kingdom of God is His priority. Jesus didn't want any delays, because people need to know about the kingdom. People need kingdom representatives who will proclaim the good news of the kingdom of heaven. People perish for lack of understanding. That's why Jesus is raising up committed kingdom followers to proclaim the gospel to everyone. This task is no small thing, and it comes with difficulties and spiritual warfare.

Anyone who is too tethered to their human relationships, even to their yesterday, has become useless for the kingdom of God. Have you ever been behind someone in line at a fast-food restaurant and they can't make up their mind on what to order? It can be very frustrating to wait on someone who goes from thing to thing to thing, never deciding what to do. They wind up delaying everyone behind them as they struggle to make a decision. Jesus knew that anyone following Him who was tied to yesterday would toggle too much in decision-making. They would need to "check on home" before heading out to follow Christ. They would want to take care of material needs before spiritual needs. All of this would delay what God was doing in advancing His kingdom.

When it comes to following Jesus Christ and advancing His kingdom agenda, you need to make up your mind and keep moving forward. There's no time to recapture the good ol' days. Discipleship is a commitment that leaves all else behind. You must make yourself fit for the kingdom. You must present yourself as someone whom God can use. Because if you're still in love with yesterday, then following God is not part of your story. Jesus wants you to follow Him, not just fit Him in.

The third man was simply double-minded. He had made a decision for God. But he had also made a decision to look back. He was trying to mix unleaded with diesel. He was listening to AM and FM at the same time. He was trying to watch Netflix, YouTube, and Hulu simultaneously. As a result, there was confusion and a lack of focus on any one thing.

SPREAD TOO THIN

Many people today lack purpose and direction in life because their focus is spread too thin. They think they have made a commitment to God, but if they were honest about it, it was just lip service. They are still looking at other options. Or looking back at how things were. The apostle Paul reminded us that looking back is no way to move forward. He said, "Brethren, I do not regard myself as having laid hold of it yet; but one thing I do: forgetting what lies behind and reaching forward to what lies ahead, I press on toward the goal for the prize of the upward call of God in Christ Jesus" (Philippians 3:13–14).

Whatever it is you have left behind, you need to forget it. Whether it is good, bad, or ugly—you need to let it go. If you've chosen to follow Jesus, the past no longer determines your decisions. Jesus determines your decisions. The past no longer holds you back. Jesus propels you forward. Whether you struggle from past pain or trauma or a series of great accomplishments or defeats, all of that needs to be surrendered at the feet of the Savior and Lord. Even though you may not know where Christ is leading you, you need to trust Him enough to follow His directions. Following Jesus and promoting the kingdom of God is an all-in process. Jesus told us more about it earlier in Luke 9:

> And He was saying to them all, "If anyone wishes to come after Me, he must deny himself, and take up his cross daily and follow Me. For whoever wishes to save his life will lose it, but whoever loses his life for My sake, he is the one who will save it. For what is a man profited if he gains the whole world, and loses or forfeits himself? For whoever is ashamed of Me and My words, the Son of Man will be ashamed of him when He comes in

> His glory, and the glory of the Father and of the holy angels. But I say to you truthfully, there are some of those standing here who will not taste death until they see the kingdom of God." (vv. 23–27)

This is the call of discipleship. This is the portrait of true commitment. Losing your life for the sake of Christ is what it takes to unleash the kingdom power of God in all you do. Following Jesus is no small thing. It's not a hobby. It's not a side hustle. Following Jesus involves a heartfelt, dedicated commitment to Him and what He says to do at all times. Far too many Christians think following Jesus is like going to an ice cream social. It's all fun and games. It's one big party. But an ice cream social is not real life. Just like the Magic Kingdom is not real life. There is one kingdom that is real; that is God's kingdom, and it's not a cotton-candy experience.

If you've chosen to follow Jesus, the past no longer determines your decisions. Jesus determines your decisions.

While there exist many benefits and blessings that come with following Jesus, there also exist difficulties and troubles. There are inconveniences. Taking a stand for Jesus means you will face problems. Taking a stand for Jesus means you will face opposition. Taking a stand for Jesus means you will suffer loss. Taking a stand for Jesus means you will not be able to look back on what was or wistfully wonder what might have been.

Unleashing the reality of the kingdom means eyes straight ahead—no matter the cost, the difficulty, the trial, or the outcome. Jesus gave the three men only two options. First, they could hear His call to follow Him and reject Him. Or they could hear His call to follow Him and then follow Him. What they could not do is negotiate the terms of following Jesus. Jesus came to earth to do the Father's business. He has a plan. As the head of the body, He leads us in that plan. That plan is nonnegotiable. It's not to be marginalized. It doesn't come as an afterthought or if you have some extra time or energy left over.

The plan of advancing God's kingdom agenda on earth is a significant and strategic plan. Casual workers won't win this battle. It comes with much opposition in spiritual warfare. Part-time or cultural Christianity won't cut it. Double-mindedness won't cut it. In fact, double-mindedness unleashes nothing at all. We read in James 1:6–8: "But he must ask in faith without any doubting, for the one who doubts is like the surf of the sea, driven and tossed by the wind. For that man ought not to expect that he will receive anything from the Lord, being a double-minded man, unstable in all his ways."

Once God sees that you are living with a double mind or a dual focus, even if you are serious about His kingdom, He says He is no longer serious about you and your role in advancing His kingdom. James made it clear that living in a dual-focused reality means you "ought not to expect that [you] will receive anything from the Lord." One of the reasons is because He doesn't know whether or not He can count on you. He doesn't know if you are going to bail on Him tomorrow. Or if you are going to take a leave of absence when things get rough. You might have your hand to the plow today, but if you live with a dual focus, there's no telling which way that plow will go. Everything you touch will wind up crooked if you don't keep your eyes straight ahead and fixed on Jesus.

THE CALL TO FIX YOUR EYES ON JESUS

Only through a steady focus on Jesus Christ will you find the strength to continue on in the daily grind of spiritual life. The writer of Hebrews put it like this:

> Therefore, since we have so great a cloud of witnesses surrounding us, let us also lay aside every encumbrance and the sin which so easily entangles us, and let us run with endurance the race that is set before us, fixing our eyes on Jesus, the author and perfecter of faith, who for the joy set before Him endured the cross, despising the shame, and has sat down at the right hand of the throne of God.
>
> For consider Him who has endured such hostility by sinners against Himself, so that you will not grow weary and lose heart. (12:1–3)

Growing weary leads to burnout. Burnout leads to quitting. Quitting accomplishes nothing in advancing God's kingdom on earth. The way you are to avoid growing weary is by fixing your eyes firmly on Jesus. He is the author of your faith. He is the perfecter of your faith. Where you are weak, He is strong. Where you lack the ability or wisdom you need, He supplies all. Following Jesus comes through focusing solely on Jesus. When you do that, you'll see heaven unleashed and the benefits of the kingdom unleashed on your behalf.

Preachers or spiritual teachers have been known to, at times, paint a one-sided picture of Christianity. They promote the good things tied to a relationship with Jesus. And while there are blessings galore to be accessed, there can also be difficulties, loss, and suffering. That's the whole story. Following Jesus involves focusing on Jesus wholeheartedly. Satan is a master at creating distractions to take our focus off Jesus. A true, committed disciple of Christ has the wisdom and wherewithal to recognize a distraction when it presents itself and to keep his or her eyes on the Lord.

One of the more popular passages in Scripture is found in Luke 14 and talks about our role in the culture and the world. It comes after Jesus told the crowds around Him that if anyone follows Him, they need to place all else after Him, including family (vv. 25–26). The passage doesn't mean you are to turn against your family or your spouse. But it does mean that if there ever is a choice between serving Christ and His kingdom and that of prioritizing your spouse or family, you are to choose Jesus. This may sound harsh, but living as a kingdom disciple who functions as a kingdom servant in order to make a kingdom impact requires a true daily commitment (Luke 9:23).

You can go to church every day the doors are open or memorize Scripture as much as you are able, but without a true commitment to following Jesus, that is just so much extra you are doing. Making a lasting impact on those around you is possible only through the unleashing of the Spirit's power from Jesus Christ. It is then that you will make a positive impact.

Jesus explained this impact in Luke 14:34–35: "Therefore, salt is good; but if even salt has become tasteless, with what will it be seasoned? It is useless either for the soil or for the manure pile; it is thrown out. He who has ears to hear, let him hear." Useless salt adds no value to whatever it touches. Similarly, useless saints add no kingdom value to whatever they touch. Anytime Christians live in such a way that God is not free to unleash His kingdom power through them, they have become useless believers as far as transformational impact is concerned. They are there and they are loved by God, yes. But if God can't utilize their time, talents, or treasures for the kingdom, then they are no better than tasteless salt. They take up space.

Or, for my football-fan friends, what good is an offensive lineman who can't block? What good is a wide receiver who can't catch? What good is a quarterback who can't throw the ball? Or we could move to another sport. What good is a baseball player who can't run? Or what about a basketball player who can't dribble? All of these players may have a uniform on, but if they can't do what the role requires them to do, then they will be off the team in no time.

If you have trusted in Jesus Christ for the forgiveness of

your sins, you are on Jesus' team. You are on Team Eternity. But if you choose not to live a life dedicated to Him with full commitment, full focus, and a willingness to keep your eyes fixed on Him, you may not be on Team Kingdom Impact. Team Kingdom Impact players are those who are specifically equipped to carry out Jesus' mission on earth, which is to bring glory to God by advancing His kingdom agenda in history. Jesus is looking for followers, not fans. He's looking for disciples, not mere devotees. He wants your commitment, not your casual association when it suits you. Bringing glory to God is your calling, and when you live out that calling, you tap into the power to fulfill what God has planned for your life. Remember, Jesus has a noncompete clause in His kingdom covenant with us.

Chapter Five

FINDING WHAT YOU'RE MEANT TO DO

Kingdom Purpose

IF YOU'VE EVER OPENED A PUZZLE BOX, YOU'VE COME INTO contact with a myriad of disconnected pieces. Each piece of the puzzle is only as significant as the degree to which it fits into a bigger picture. On its own, each puzzle piece has not discovered its purpose for existence. The purpose for the piece is the picture. The purpose for the piece is never the piece itself. A puzzle piece on its own makes no picture at all.

But when the piece connects with the other pieces, it creates a fuller expression of the design. It contributes to a greater glory of the image itself.

When we fixate on ourselves, our goals, and our choices alone, we fail to create the fuller expression of design that brings God glory.

We are made in the image of God as individuals. But when we fixate on ourselves, our goals, and our choices alone, we fail to create the fuller expression of design that brings God glory. You and I are a part of a bigger picture. You are not the picture itself. Neither am I. There is a bigger picture taking place, putting God's glory on display. If and when you miss that goal and meaning for your life, you will also miss your reason for being: We are created to connect. The apostle Peter expressed it like this: "And coming to Him as to a living stone which has been rejected by men, but is choice and precious in the sight of God, you also, as living stones, are being built up as a spiritual house for a holy priesthood, to offer up spiritual sacrifices acceptable to God through Jesus Christ" (1 Peter 2:4–5).

Examine any home or building constructed of rock or stone and you'll see more than a single rock or stone. The building became a building because of the joining together of rock or stone. Without the individual rocks or stones joining in the process of construction, there would be no building. Similarly, each of us in the body of Christ has a part to play in a greater creation story. As we discover how to set aside our individual desires and look instead to the greater collective good through the glorifying of God, we build a spiritual house through Jesus Christ.

Unfortunately, many people today spend their lives climbing the so-called ladder of success only to discover, when they reach the top, that the ladder was leaning against the wrong wall. They may have gotten to the top only to find out there isn't anything there. Others spend their lives on a treadmill called "busy," always moving but never arriving anywhere meaningful. What God is seeking in each of us, as pieces of His kingdom puzzle, is our involvement in a cohesive purpose called *His kingdom agenda.* We are to come together as His greater image.

God has one overarching picture and purpose for our existence: the advancement of His kingdom and glory on earth. When God's kingdom agenda advances, His glory becomes magnified. God's divine authority, expressed through everyday life, brings Him the greatest glory.

God's goal when creating history and time (since He exists outside of history and time) was to implant and expand the imprint of His heavenly realm in this earthly realm. The message of the Lord's Prayer emphasizes this when we pray: "Your kingdom come. Your will be done, on earth as it is in heaven" (Matthew 6:10). The creation of humanity helped in delivering the divine will of the heavenly kingdom into an earthly environment. The heavenly kingdom exists as a spiritual realm, yet the earthly plane involves the physical. Physical people, thus, are to carry out the unseen spiritual plan of God's kingdom in an environment that we can see and experience.

Our part in this divinely orchestrated cosmic puzzle called life rests in participating in extracting the will of God from heaven and implementing it in history. Anything you or I do that does not flow with God's will is operating outside of our created purpose. When you understand and accept the reality that you were made on purpose and for a purpose, it changes your whole outlook on life. It affects your ambitions. It narrows your focus. It even adjusts how you schedule your time and utilize your talents. What's more, it helps you identify the existence of a rival kingdom headed by Satan, which seeks to knock you off the divine purpose God has planned. This "kingdom of darkness" wants nothing more than to deactivate, defeat, or demoralize you on your path toward pursuing your purpose.

RECOGNIZING THE RIVAL KINGDOM

The kingdom of darkness could be compared to the ants you see crawling in your yard. You may see only a few ants at a time, but if you were to trace them back to their anthill, you would discover an entire kingdom of ants underground. Because of the strength and sheer volume of ants in this underground kingdom, they are difficult to destroy. They also take great delight in destroying your yard in service to their queen. They will not hold back when it comes to growing and nurturing their own kingdom beneath your grass.

The ant illustration serves as a visual example of the kingdom of darkness. There exists a rival spiritual kingdom out of sight that seeks to steer you away from your greatest good. The devil and his minions lurk in places we cannot identify, looking to trip us up and remove us from the fulfillment of God's plan. Satan acts like a bitter ex bent on destroying all hope of good in the life of the one he lost. This is because you and I once belonged to his kingdom, but through the shed blood of Jesus Christ, we have been redeemed and rescued from it. We read in Colossians 1:13–14: "For He rescued us from the domain of darkness, and transferred us to the kingdom of His beloved Son, in whom we have redemption, the forgiveness of sins."

You no longer belong to Satan or his domain of darkness, and he feels jilted as a result. He will do everything in his power, using deception as his primary tool, to upend your plans and distract you from pursuing God's way for you. That's why it is critical to recognize the bigger picture you have been designed to create. Because if you see only the pains, challenges, difficulties, or desires in your life, you may find it easier to give up or give in to Satan's schemes. Yet when you realize how you affect the lives of those around you for good or for bad, it provides the motivation to overcome. Seeing the bigger picture enables you to understand what your goal is and to press on toward that goal.

Very few people watch sporting events on a small-screen television in their kitchen. This is because most kitchen televisions are placed there to give you an opportunity to glance at it while you are doing other things. Most people watch sporting events in their living room or media room. They want to focus on the game. They want to see every play. A television in the kitchen won't do because people have other reasons for being there—usually to cook or to eat.

That's pretty easy to understand. But what many Christians fail to understand today is that too many of us are tuning in to God's will and His Word from the kitchen of our lives. We give God a glance while we do other things. We have God turned on in the background only to wonder why we keep getting defeated by Satan so easily. God wants and deserves to be the centerpiece of your days. He requires your focus. If you miss the centrality of why you are here—the bigger picture—you miss out on unleashing His kingdom purpose, authority, and grace to carry out your purpose.

You have a part to play in God's overarching kingdom image. Just like no other human has your fingerprints, no other puzzle piece has your design.

If railroad cars are not linked to the engine, they will fail to go anywhere. Even if these railroad cars contain very valuable things, they will not reach their destination unless they are attached to the engine. Similarly, you contain many valuable things within you—these are talents, gifts, and ways to bring about good in this world. But you will not arrive at your intended destinations to do so unless you connect to the engine of Jesus Christ as Lord. That's why the Enemy seeks to steer you away from Jesus. That's why the Enemy seeks to distract you from living out your purpose. That's why Satan seeks to stifle your ability to grow and actively engage culture with your matured spiritual gifts. You have a part to play in God's overarching kingdom image. Just like no other human has your fingerprints, no other puzzle piece has your design.

RENEWING YOUR MINDSET

God has a unique purpose for your life, but in order to discover and maximize it, you need to start thinking with a kingdom mindset. A lot of attention is drawn to this idea of having the right mindset these days. People talk a lot about making time to think or living with a healthy mindset. But having the right mindset is nothing new. God has called us all to live with a divine mindset. We see this in the following passages:

> Whether, then, you eat or drink or whatever you do, do all to the glory of God. (1 Corinthians 10:31)

> For who has known the mind of the Lord, that he will instruct Him? But we have the mind of Christ. (1 Corinthians 2:16)

> Do nothing from selfishness or empty conceit, but with humility of mind regard one another as more important than yourselves; do not merely look out for your own personal interests, but also for the interests of others. Have this attitude in yourselves which was also in Christ Jesus,

> who, although He existed in the form of God, did not regard equality with God a thing to be grasped, but emptied Himself, taking the form of a bond-servant, and being made in the likeness of men. Being found in appearance as a man, He humbled Himself by becoming obedient to the point of death, even death on a cross. (Philippians 2:3–8)

> Therefore I urge you, brethren, by the mercies of God, to present your bodies a living and holy sacrifice, acceptable to God, which is your spiritual service of worship. And do not be conformed to this world, but be transformed by the renewing of your mind, so that you may prove what the will of God is, that which is good and acceptable and perfect. (Romans 12:1–2)

It's the renewing of your mind that produces life transformation. As your mindset renews to align with God's kingdom mindset, you'll live out your intended purpose. Whether in eating, drinking, or in whatever you are doing, when you live with a kingdom mindset, you do each thing for God's glory.

We often make the mistake of dividing spiritual activities from physical, more human activities. But 1 Corinthians 10:31 tells us that, for God, there is no such thing as an unspiritual activity. There are no mundane things to do. Even if it is only washing the dishes or vacuuming the floor or taking out the trash, it is to be done for God's glory. How many times have you considered how to take out the trash in a way that glorifies God? I would encourage you to give that consideration. God has asked us to live and function with a kingdom mindset that makes His glory our goal. We are to seek the advancement of God's kingdom in all we do.

As we've seen in earlier chapters, the kingdom refers to the jurisdiction, the rule of God. As Psalm 24:1 tells us, that jurisdiction applies to everything: "The earth is the Lord's, and all it contains, the world, and those who dwell in it." God claims a monopoly on His creation. Not only that, but He has a plan for His creation—every single piece, part, and person.

You are God's "workmanship." Another way to say that is you are God's unique work of art. You work for God. Ephesians 2:8–10 summarizes His plan for each of us: "For by grace you have been saved through faith; and that not of yourselves, it is the gift of God; not as a result of works, so that no one may boast. For we are His workmanship, created in Christ Jesus for good works, which God prepared beforehand so that we would walk in them." He created and converted you as His worker in a world that needs to be touched and transformed by His glory. We become a disappointment when we are not fulfilling that purpose. You have been custom-made for kingdom impact.

You have been custom-made for kingdom impact.

THE DISCIPLINE OF ALIGNMENT

No appliance decides what it wants to be. No piece of technology decides what it wants to be. The manufacturer decides what does what. The creator decides the toaster will be used to toast. The toaster doesn't speak into that at all. The moment the toaster tries to refrigerate bread instead of make toast, it is the moment the toaster is either tossed or repaired.

Likewise, you and I have been designed in a unique way for the good works God wants us to carry out. He's given you gifts that benefit not only yourself but the collective. He's given you treasures that you can enjoy, but they are also meant to be shared and to help others. The moment you begin living for you rather than living for God is the moment you, like the toaster, start refrigerating the bread instead of toasting it. God desires everything you do to be done for His glory and according to the purposes He has intended for you all along.

The problems come when we try to refrigerate the bread that's meant to be toasted. That's when God, in His great wisdom and mercy, will often allow things in our lives to get shaken so that we get back in alignment with Him. He takes us to His toolshed to sort things out. Hebrews 12 talks about the discipline process believers sometimes face:

> It is for discipline that you endure; God deals with you as with sons; for what son is there whom his father does not discipline? But if you are without discipline, of which all have become partakers, then you are illegitimate children and not sons. Furthermore, we had earthly fathers to discipline us, and we respected them; shall we not much rather be subject to the Father of spirits, and live? For they disciplined us for a short time as seemed best to them, but He disciplines us for our good, so that we may share His

> holiness. All discipline for the moment seems not to be joyful, but sorrowful; yet to those who have been trained by it, afterwards it yields the peaceful fruit of righteousness. (vv. 7–11)

God does correct and perfect us through His discipline. At other times, He allows challenges in our lives to shake us up so that we will look to and come to fully know the stability He supplies. When we live our lives in alignment under His rule, we can rest in His power, peace, and security no matter what goes on around us. That doesn't mean everything will always go smoothly. What it does mean is that we will know and abide in the One who remains unaffected by the shaking going on. Hebrews 12 describes God's unshakable kingdom in this way:

> See to it that you do not refuse Him who is speaking. For if those did not escape when they refused him who warned them on earth, much less will we escape who turn away from Him who warns from heaven. And His voice shook the earth then, but now He has promised, saying, "Yet once more I will shake not only the earth, but also the heaven." This expression, "Yet once more," denotes the removing of those things which can be shaken, as of created things, so that those things which cannot be shaken may remain. Therefore, since we receive a kingdom which cannot be shaken, let us show gratitude, by which we may offer to God an acceptable service with reverence and awe; for our God is a consuming fire. (vv. 25–29)

In this passage we see the contrast between things that are able to be shaken and that which is unshakable. The word *shake* means to disturb the natural order of things. It indicates a disturbance of peace and function. When God either shakes or allows the natural order of things to be shaken, it's because He wants you to pay close attention to Him and His kingdom program. It means He has something to say. He wants all eyes on Him. He wants you to listen to Him.

Have you ever been on an airplane that encountered some severe turbulence? The plane bounces around like a toy in the sky. People start grabbing their armrests, gripping until their knuckles turn white. Then, to everyone's relief, a voice comes over the intercom. It's the voice of the pilot. All talking instantly stops. Whoever was watching a movie or listening to music pulls out their earbuds. Everyone focuses on the voice of the captain because everyone wants to know what he has to say about the shaking. If his voice and his words assure you that you'll be out of the rough air soon, you can see fingers loosen their grip and stress melt off the faces of those who were once concerned. This is because the captain has spoken.

God will either allow or create turbulent times in our lives and circumstances in order to get our attention. He will do this so we will listen attentively to Him. If we are too busy watching movies, playing video games, or listening to music that we tune Him out when He speaks, He knows how to make us listen. He knows how to shift our focus from whatever it was on back to Him. Thus, instead of getting mad at

God, get glad. He allows these disturbances to get us back on track.

Most of the time people ignore the weather report. But when a major storm approaches, all eyes and ears are on the meteorologists. We listen because we want to know how bad it's going to get, how long it's going to last, whether schools and businesses will be shut down, and so much more. We listen because our world is being disrupted by a storm. God wants us to listen to Him too. And when we won't listen, He has been known to create or allow a storm to get our undivided attention.

Not only does He allow shaking to take place in order to get our attention, but the passage from Hebrews 12 reveals He also allows or creates shaking in order to remove that which can be shaken. He's getting rid of that which wouldn't stand the test. He's trying to replace something tangible and uncertain with something that can last. Unfortunately, we get too attached to the tangible realities in our lives. We get too connected so that they become a barrier to living out our kingdom calling. In those situations, God will remove our attachments from us in order to detach us from that which prevents us from pursuing His kingdom plan. Our ultimate obligation is always to God. When we make our obligations about something other than God, He will often remove them from our lives altogether. What's worse, that may hurt.

If an earthquake happened while an airplane flew over at thirty-five thousand feet in the sky, no one in the plane would feel the earthquake. That's because the plane would not be attached to the land in any way. It's the things that

God wants us to listen to Him too. And when we won't listen, He has been known to create or allow a storm to get our undivided attention.

are attached that get shaken in an earthquake. What God wants to do is lift us up to a new spiritual reality of a kingdom that is not attached to this world. He doesn't want you to get "shook up" when this world experiences the chaos it frequently does. When you attach yourself to God and His kingdom, you will withstand the challenges of this world because you will have unleashed His rule within you. Your connection to God stabilizes you because His kingdom cannot be shaken. Now, that doesn't mean the circumstances and trials aren't real. It just means they no longer dominate or control you. They no longer dictate your emotions or your decisions. They no longer call the shots.

GRATITUDE IN THE STORM

Did you know that no matter how hard it rains on the ocean, the rain can only penetrate the ocean so far? Even in a torrential downpour, the rain can only go so deep. That's why fish know to swim to a certain depth in a storm and wait it out. The fish know the storm will not affect them where they are. There may be waves as tall as skyscrapers up near the top of the ocean, but down below it is calm. In other words, when life gets stormy, it's an indication to go deeper with God. And one of the ways you go deeper with God is revealed to us in Hebrews 12:28: "Therefore, since we receive a kingdom which cannot be shaken, let us show gratitude, by which we may offer to God an acceptable service with reverence and awe." You go deeper with God by showing gratitude. Thankfulness invites God's peace into your soul, especially during difficult seasons.

That doesn't mean you need to be thankful for the difficulties or pains that you face. What it means is that you need to be thankful that God is doing something, saying something, or creating something in the midst of the chaos. You are thankful that God is drawing you nearer to Him. You don't thank God for the problem, but you thank Him for the purpose. Thank Him for revealing to you what true peace and purpose really are. Thank Him for reminding you where to focus. Thank Him for showing you that He can take a mess and make a miracle.

But for Him to do so, you need to listen for His voice. You need to look for His hand. You need to rest in His peace and unleash His grace. The apostle Paul knew about the process of unleashing grace:

> Because of the surpassing greatness of the revelations, for this reason, to keep me from exalting myself, there was given me a thorn in the flesh, a messenger of Satan to torment me—to keep me from exalting myself! Concerning this I implored the Lord three times that it might leave me. And He has said to me, "My grace is sufficient for you, for power is perfected in weakness." Most gladly, therefore, I will rather boast about my weaknesses, so that the power of Christ may dwell in me. Therefore I am well content with weaknesses, with insults, with distresses, with persecutions, with difficulties, for Christ's sake; for when I am weak, then I am strong. (2 Corinthians 12:7–10)

For God to unleash His grace in our lives often means we are facing some difficult times. But that's when you discover how strong you really are, because when you are weak, the power of Christ dwells in you to make you strong. Paul's thorn in his flesh led him not only to a place of surrender but also to a place of gratitude. He realized the benefits that came through the difficulties he faced. This then propelled him to a greater level of service, due to his deeper experience of God's grace.

The writer of Hebrews extolled us to offer a similar level of "acceptable service" for the grace and peace we've been given. We read this earlier in Hebrews 12:28: "Offer to God an acceptable service with reverence and awe." God has so fashioned you for service. He is not looking for Christian celebrities; He's looking for kingdom servants. Whatever grace, gifts, talents, or treasures He has given to you, they have been given so you can serve Him. It's as simple as that. When you choose to use God's gifts to focus solely on yourself, you may find yourself in a situation similar to Paul's. He acknowledged he was given a thorn so that he would not exalt himself. He was given a thorn so that he would remember why he was created and gifted in his life. He was created for service and good works to benefit the greater good of the body of Christ while advancing God's kingdom on earth.

Your life is about more than just you. God wants you to know you have a part to play in the collective drama taking place. You are a piece of the puzzle, not the puzzle itself. Unleashing His power in your life comes through recognizing your connection to His body and your role in it. When you do that, you will tap into a deeper level of grace, stability, and strength than you've ever known before. You will begin to see your contribution to the tapestry of God's kingdom image on earth.

Paul's concluding statement is that our God is a consuming fire (Hebrews 12:29). Like ironing is designed to remove wrinkles from clothing, God shakes out our wrinkles to remove that which is unacceptable to Him and His purpose for us because He wants His glory to look good on us as we serve His unshakable kingdom.

Chapter Six

GROUNDED IN WHAT MATTERS MOST

Kingdom Truth

ONE OF THE WAYS I CREATIVELY PROVIDED FOR MY FAMILY during my seminary years was through house-sitting. This was not only a great source of income, but it enabled me to stay with my family while we earned it. Even more, the people we house-sat for typically lived in very large homes in the Highland Park area of Dallas, and they left the fridge stocked with food. One time the owner even offered his

Bentley for me to drive to and from Dallas Theological Seminary. You know he didn't have to tell me twice! I drove that Bentley slow enough for everyone to catch a glimpse, getting out of it even more slowly when I parked. There were many perks that came with house-sitting.

There were also guidelines given to govern what we did and how things were handled during the family's physical absence from their home. Whether it was guidelines for the care of their kids or the care of their pets or for the upkeep of the yard and the home, we were always given a set of instructions before we arrived. These instructions included certain allowances, restrictions, and an overall set of expectations we were to abide by in their home. When we received these instructions, we understood it was just part of the role. We didn't negotiate with the homeowners. We didn't complain about the instructions. We were guests in someone else's home and hired to steward it in their absence. We knew their guidelines were part of the process of stewarding their resources, and we were getting paid to do it. If we wanted to stay in their house, then we lived under their jurisdiction.

As we are seeing during our time in this book, God has a sphere of jurisdiction called His kingdom. It's the sphere of His authority from which He operates. From Genesis to Revelation we read about His rule and authority. It involves the space He occupies in order to carry out and advance His will. Located within this jurisdiction are His governance and guidelines. We often refer to this as truth. They are the expectations in which we are to operate.

For example, one expectation in God's physical realm is gravity. You can't negotiate with gravity. If you try, you'll soon discover that gravity is the better negotiator. God's guidelines are nonnegotiable. He has set up His universe to function according to an exact and precise manner. But God has not left us in the dark when it comes to how we can operate in His realm. He has given us His guidelines (whether spiritual, physical, emotional, or other) so that we can best function as kingdom stewards. He's given His truth for our benefit. Whether or not you learn it or apply it is up to you, but He has given it for your good as well as the greater good of all involved. Abiding under His rule produces well-being. Deviating from His rule produces problems.

When God's truth becomes sidelined, we face the consequences. You may have witnessed this in your own life or in the lives of those you love. It's very easy to witness this in the culture at large. That's why God's goal for His kingdom people is for us to be people of the truth. We are not to be people of our truth or even a person of my truth. We are to be people of the truth. When we are, we will impart the goodness of God to a world in need. Standing for the truth and spreading principles of truth is essential when you follow Jesus Christ.

God's goal for His kingdom people is for us to be people of the truth. We are not to be people of our truth or even a person of my truth. We are to be people of the truth.

A WORLD IN CHAOS WITHOUT TRUTH

Yet, as I'm sure you know, the truth is rarely a popular concept. We find it under attack in our contemporary culture every single day. People debate truth. People argue for tolerance, tolerating everything but the truth. Our culture resembles the biblical times recorded in the book of Judges: "In those days there was no king in Israel; every man did what was right in his own eyes" (17:6). Chaos is the natural result of confusion regarding truth. The devolution of society stems from the failure to abide by a divinely set standard.

But not only was truth questioned in the time of the Old Testament; it was also under attack in the time of the New Testament. Even in Jesus' day, truth came under fire. We see this with the Roman governor Pontius Pilate, who asked Jesus, "What is truth?" (John 18:38). Pilate didn't ask that question in search of a real answer. It was a rhetorical question. He was making the point that nobody agrees on truth. Nobody is on the same page. Nobody adheres to a set standard by which reality is to be measured. Pilate put forth the one truth most people could agree on: There exists no solid truth system. Rather, most people believe we exist within a multiplicity of -isms that frame our experiences.

Pragmatism relies on what works right now. Positivism allows for science-backed truth, understanding that science changes and evolves. Relativism refers to truth that we can logically deduce. Agnosticism means we just don't know and can't know truth. All of the -isms create a thought construct that rests in the subjective and malleable personal experiences of humanity, both individually and collectively. In this set of constructs, people scurry about to define, rewrite, discover, tweak, or bend truth to fit their agendas.

This often elevates the voices of the masses, depending on which particular interest or focus a person may have. Many people are addicted to podcasts in their search for some form of truth. We have babble-by-the-hour available on every topic imaginable these days. Social media channels consume people's days and nights. We are awash today in opinions purported to be truth. What's more, as belief systems change and shift based on more information or new information or new ideas or the whim of the moment, people tune in repeatedly to hear the newest set of truth structures on which to base their lives. Thus, we are consumed with chaos.

Philosophical chaos erupts as people doodle with ideas about the meaning of our existence as well as the construct of our existence. Questions on human origins no longer focus on evolution. We have more questions now, such as are we in a hologram, simulation, or a parallel universe? Theatrical releases and streaming shows emphasize these options over and over in our collective thought bubble.

We also wrestle with ongoing social chaos because we can't seem to arrive at a truth on social issues, race, class, or culture. Gender chaos has also taken a front seat in a confused world bent on redefining the biology of humanity.

Much of the questions in these areas feed into a greater level of psychological chaos as well. People struggle to understand their identity and emotions. This feeds into both moral and spiritual chaos or vice versa. People are perpetually looking to polls to find out what percentage of individuals agree with them, as if margins somehow determine truth. It's a never-ending cycle of confusion, bringing 2 Timothy 3:7 into full light: "Always learning and never able to come to the knowledge of the truth."

Our colleges and universities contribute to educating ourselves into various levels of craziness, because when education lacks a defining line of truth, it aims at any moving targets. I've met plenty of educators with doctorates who don't seem to know the first thing about truth. Maybe you have too. Reality, subjects, and study fluctuate when trust no longer exists to guide them. Yet, when it comes down to it, we all intuitively understand the need for truth.

What would you say to an unsure pilot who announces to the passengers that he's going to guess at what buttons to push to get to their collective destination? Or what about pharmacists who disagree with your doctor's prescription and give you what they feel like instead? What about surgeons who guess where to make an opening incision based on the latest poll? None of us want a lack of truth when it comes to areas in our lives like these. We need truth as a standard for living and functioning at every level, but some levels are more obvious than others.

When our perception of what we believe to be truth is based on emotion, this so-called body of truth can only vacillate with the moment. In one moment, we hear it is good to eat meat. In the next moment, we hear it is not good to eat meat. In one moment, eating eggs is healthy. In the next, eating eggs is unhealthy. Stuff keeps changing because information and opinion, as well as influences such as corporate greed, continually change.

More than that, though, stuff can change based on who you talk to. What may be right for one is wrong for another. What may be wrong for one is right for another. Ask ten people the same question and you'll likely get ten different answers, even with each answer being rooted in truth. Issues arise for believers, though, when we listen to the world's version of truth—or even our own—above God's. When we start to ask the question like Pilate did concerning truth, or we start to do what is right in our own eyes, we will face the consequences of deviating from divinely revealed truth.

THE UNWAVERING TRUTH OF GOD'S WORD

Unleashing God's kingdom in your life and through your life to impact others cannot be done apart from an awareness of and an abiding with truth. That's why determining truth based on God's Word is so important. Similarly, making distinctions between spiritual truth and worldly wisdom is critical. Jesus made the statement, which led to Pilate's now-infamous question, that He does not belong to this world. He rules and reigns from another realm. We read in John 18:36: "My kingdom is not of this world. If My kingdom were of this world, then My servants would be fighting so that I would not be handed over to the Jews; but as it is, My kingdom is not of this realm."

Unleashing God's kingdom in your life and through your life to impact others cannot be done apart from an awareness of and an abiding with truth.

The primary principle in understanding truth begins with knowing from where Jesus rules and reigns. His home base, His place of operation, is not of this world. It is in the world but it is not of this world. It is sourced from another realm. Thus, since Jesus is "the truth" (John 14:6), any discussion of truth cannot start from this realm we know as earth. The spiritual must always inform the physical, not the other way around. The kingdom on high must inform the life here. The invisible world must inform the world of the five senses, because truth is derived from the heavenly realm. Anytime we try to establish a truth based on the realities of our existence, we are unable to come to the whole truth. We lack the necessary components and information to determine truth here on earth. Truth is established by God and given to us on earth. Yet, even so, our society desires and even attempts to impose its rules on God's house, and then we wonder why so much conflict exists.

Truth is defined as the absolute standard by which reality is measured. Truth is God's view on any subject. The reason this is so is because God alone is perfect. Perfection can't make a mistake on any subject or else it's no longer perfect. The apostle Paul put it this way: "Let God be found true, though every man be found a liar" (Romans 3:4). Whenever you disagree with God, you're wrong. Whenever your social circle disagrees with God, they are wrong. Whenever your professor, pastor, or boss disagrees with God, they are wrong. Whenever politicians disagree with God, they are wrong. Whenever economists disagree with God, they are wrong. There exist two answers to every question: God's and everyone else's. When everyone else disagrees with God, they are wrong. Truth exists as an absolute standard.

A university professor was arguing that there was no such thing as absolute truth. A clever student raised his hand and asked, "Do you believe what you are saying absolutely?"

Until your view of truth aligns with that derived from the spiritual standard of God and His kingdom jurisdiction, you will be bound in a confusion of thought. Hosea 4:6 records the results like this: "My people are destroyed for lack of knowledge. Because you have rejected knowledge." The physical world exists only because the spiritual world made it.

A pot can't tell the potter the truth of how it came to be. Only the craftsman who molded the clay knows the story. We have great audacity to try to tell God the truth by which this world operates or should operate. God alone knows the truth. If we were wise, we would make pursuing God our highest goal. Truth is revealed through an intimate and abiding relationship with God through His Son, Jesus Christ.

Let's look at another example. Suppose you didn't agree that one plus one equals two. Your agreement is irrelevant in the world of mathematics. The fact that you may not like or appreciate one plus one equaling two doesn't matter. Even the fact that your mom or dad may have told you when you were very young that one plus one does not equal two does not change the reality that one plus one equals two. It has always equaled two. It will always equal two. No matter how committed you may be to your emotions that become troubled or traumatized by one plus one equaling two, it does not validate anything other than your emotions being out of sync with truth. Truth overrules emotion in the overarching operation of our reality.

Another thing to keep in mind when examining the importance of truth in unleashing God's kingdom benefits in your life is the fact that truth goes deeper than facts. Facts can tell you a lot. But they will often not tell you the whole truth. For example, you may have a headache. Having a headache is a fact. To address this fact, you may take a pain reliever only to discover that your head still hurts. Next, you decide to go to the doctor because there has to be more to this headache than just pain. That's when the doctor uncovers more facts—a tumor in your brain that is compressing your circulation, causing extreme pain. Over-the-counter pain medication may work well for a normal headache, but it's going to do very little for a brain tumor.

Facts are important, but we must be careful to avoid drawing conclusions or assumptions based on facts alone. As finite beings, our awareness and understanding of facts is limited. Yet, even so, there exists a large number of people in our world today who operate solely on the facts they know. All the while, they miss the greater truth that could position them for a greater experience of life.

Without truth, many people try to solve issues without getting to the root of the issues themselves. They try to mask their pain with pain medication, not realizing there is a deeper source of pain that needs to be addressed. Truth always goes deeper than facts, and how you approach whatever situation you are facing ought to be reliant on truth, not only on the facts you know.

JESUS IS THE SOURCE OF ALL TRUTH

Jesus is the source of all truth. We read that He came to testify to what is truth in the verse preceding Pilate's question: "Therefore Pilate said to Him, 'So You are a king?' Jesus answered, 'You say correctly that I am a king. For this I have been born, and for this I have come into the world, to testify to the truth. Everyone who is of the truth hears My voice'" (John 18:37). Jesus' own voice is truth itself.

He told us in John 14:6, "I am the way, and the truth, and the life; no one comes to the Father but through Me." Jesus is truth. He speaks to us through His Word, which is also perfect truth. All subjects are to be viewed and analyzed and all conclusions drawn based on Jesus Christ and His Word. Truth does not start, continue, or end anywhere else. The Bible is the voice of God in print. Yet so few people look to Jesus and His inerrant Word to reveal truth. Jesus is often an afterthought, not the primary point of reference. In fact, there are times when Jesus isn't even invited into the discussion.

We live in a cancel culture. If a person says something that goes against the powers that be, they can get shut down. One of my messages on social media was taken down because I said something that offended the online thought police. Even though what I said agreed with Scripture, it did not agree with what the culture wanted to promote. What I want to emphasize to you as you go through life is that scriptural truth cannot be canceled. It may be attacked. It may be struck down. But it cannot be canceled.

God will find a way to raise truth up from the ashes time and time again. John 10:35 states, "The Scripture cannot be broken." Scripture cannot be annulled. It cannot be canceled. Truth reigns supreme, whether acknowledged or not. Just as gravity cannot be tweaked or reduced in its influence, neither can all truth that comes from God Himself and His kingdom jurisdiction. God's truth will always win out. If it were ever canceled, the world would be canceled along with it. Physics itself depends and operates on God's truth.

Therefore, if you are a worldly Christian, you would be canceling your own spiritual growth and development. You would be annulling your own kingdom impact. You would not experience the full engagement of God in your life or the unleashing of His perfect will in you and through you.

The book of Proverbs reminds us of the validity of God's Word: "Every word of God is tested; He is a shield to those who take refuge in Him" (30:5). You can rely on God's Word. You can count on it. But if you are to wander away from it and the guiding principles His truth supplies, you can also count on inviting chaos into your life. Whether that shows

You can rely on God's Word. You can count on it. But if you are to wander away from it and the guiding principles His truth supplies, you can also count on inviting chaos into your life.

up in your personal life or your family, community, or even the world, chaos follows a departure from truth.

Amos 8:11–14 speaks to this chaotic environment that exists in the absence of God's Word:

> "Behold, days are coming," declares the
> Lord God,
> "When I will send a famine on the land,
> not a famine for bread or a thirst for water,
> but rather for hearing the words of
> the Lord.
> People will stagger from sea to sea
> and from the north even to the east;
> they will go to and fro to seek the word of
> the Lord,
> but they will not find it.
> In that day the beautiful virgins
> and the young men will faint from thirst.
> As for those who swear by the guilt of
> Samaria,
> Who say, 'As your god lives, O Dan,'
> and, 'As the way of Beersheba lives,'
> They will fall and not rise again."

We see in these verses that a famine from the Word of God led to a famine for the people in every area of their lives. When truth is abandoned, trouble quickly fills the void. Conflict and confusion fill the space left open. Disorder becomes the law of the land. And the devil has a party with the people of Christ. The devil has his way with the world's systems. The devil's number one weapon—deception—is set loose to destroy.

Prioritizing the discovery, understanding, and application of truth has to be a way of life for every follower of Jesus Christ. Now, it might not be easy. It might not be popular. But it will unleash the rule of Christ in your soul so much that even when you take a hit for standing on the truth of God's Word, you will still stand strong.

I often speak to different NFL teams during their chapel time before a game. I enjoy this opportunity to encourage these men to play with all of their hearts, to trust God, and to honor Him in what they do. But one thing I'm always reminded of when I talk to these players is that there are three teams on the field. Most people think there are just two. But the team of officials plays just as large a part in any game as the other two teams. How they rule, for good or for bad, often determines outcomes. Now, when referees make a call that a home crowd doesn't appreciate, you can bet they will hear about it. They will be booed. Just like if they make a call that the home crowd likes, they will be cheered.

Referees have a difficult job because they cannot allow the boos or the cheers to sway their calls. Their job is to stand on the truth of the rule book that governs the game. If referees were to take sides with a particular team and start making calls for one team and not the other, they would quickly be out of a job. This is because the referees' job is to remain neutral. Their job is to allow the other two teams to play a fair game based on predetermined rules. Thus, even if referees hear a cacophony of boos and jeers for making an unpopular call, that is not supposed to affect the call. The flag is not to be picked up due to a change of mind. Even if the player who was penalized gets in their face to dispute the call, the referees are to stand on the truth and on the rule or infraction called.

Similarly, you and I are to live our lives based on the rule book of God's Word. That means even if we get booed or jeered because what we do or say isn't popular with the hometown crowd here on earth, we are to stick with the truth. We are not to adjust or adapt the truth to what the world says. Rather, we are to influence the world in a way that they see the benefit of living according to the Word of God themselves.

The Word of God is the absolute standard of rule we are to live by. Just as I was given a set of rules to govern my family's time when we house-sat during my seminary years, God has given us rules to govern our time as we steward the earth made by Him. God's Word governs all. He has shown us what is good and what is not good. He has given us the "cheat code," so to speak, on how to live productive, meaningful lives. What's more, His Word doesn't change. We don't have to listen to the latest podcast or look for when God is going to upload His newest YouTube video in order to gain insight into the latest truth. Matthew 5:18 clearly states, "For truly I say to you, until heaven and earth pass away, not the smallest letter or stroke shall pass from the Law until all is accomplished." Nothing that has been revealed by God shall pass away or fail. In fact, if only one thing failed, the whole world system and planetary system would fail. All of God's truth is needed in order to maintain our elements of existence.

If you want to unleash God's involvement, tenacity, and empowering wisdom in your life, you must center yourself and your thoughts on His kingdom and His truth.

Truth is no small thing. Living your life as a person of truth is no small thing. Standing up for truth is no small thing. Basing your decisions and even your thoughts on truth is no small thing. It is the very source of life itself. That's why adopting a kingdom worldview helps you to fulfill your divine destiny. Living according to a kingdom perspective helps unleash God's favor so you can carry out your purpose. His truth is the blueprint and the building blocks for your life. Thus, if you want to unleash God's involvement, tenacity, and empowering wisdom in your life, you must center yourself and your thoughts on His kingdom and His truth.

THE POWER OF APPLYING GOD'S TRUTH

Receiving and applying the truth enables you to maximize who you are in Christ. The apostle Paul knew about the truth's work in people's lives and wrote about it to the church at Thessalonica: "For this reason we also constantly thank God that when you received the word of God which you heard from us, you accepted it not as the word of men, but for what it really is, the word of God, which also performs its work in you who believe" (1 Thessalonians 2:13). When you hear and receive truth, it performs the work in you. You don't have to stress or strain. It is the truth of God that does the work. But you must receive it.

Far too many believers are like the crumpled dollar bill that a child tries to stick into a vending machine. The wrinkled currency has nothing for the machine to hold on to, so it just spits it out. No matter how many times the child sticks the crumpled dollar bill into the machine, it will only be rejected. What's more, the kid won't get any candy, because it was the dollar bill that was supposed to do the work.

When Christians fail to understand and apply the truth of the Word of God in their lives, the chaos produces a crumpling effect on their souls. Then when they try to carry out the work and will of God, they discover they lack the power to do so. It is the truth itself that empowers you. The truth "performs its work in you" (v. 13). The truth makes the crooked places straight (Isaiah 45:2). The truth smooths out the edges. The truth causes the gears to grind and delivers the things you need to be nourished, refreshed, and strengthened. Hearing the truth isn't enough though. You need to embrace it. You must receive it. You must operate by it.

What if my late wife, Lois, and I merely read the house-sitting rules when we arrived at the home but did not adhere to them? Do you think we would be hired again? What if we told the owners that we read them, we just didn't follow them? Do you think we would have been paid? It's doubtful. Rules mean nothing when they are not followed. Hearing God's Word and applying God's Word are two vastly different things. It is in the application of the Word of God that the unleashing of the power of God takes place.

The Urban Alternative, which is the ministry I started more than four decades ago, seeks to broadcast my messages around the world. To do that, we have a vision statement. A vision statement simply defines the purpose of a ministry. In our vision statement, I wanted to clearly communicate that we were not solely a ministry for teaching the Word of God. I wanted to be sure we emphasized that we are a ministry that seeks to help people apply the Word of God. Our vision statement says: "The Urban Alternative exists in order to transform individuals, families, churches, and communities through the teaching and application of the Word of God."

Applying truth principles to your decisions matters. Applying God's rules to your life makes all the difference. Simply showing up at church to hear a sermon will do nothing for you unless you receive the truth and apply it. Just like receiving a prescription from your doctor will not help you if you do not take the medication as directed, receiving God's Word without applying it produces no results. It goes in one ear and out the other. It is the application of truth that unleashes you to experience your greatest spiritual self. This is why James said we are to be "doers of the word, and not merely hearers" (James 1:22).

Juneteenth is now a national holiday in the United States. It recognizes the time when the last slaves were notified of their freedom. Even though the Emancipation Proclamation was signed by Abraham Lincoln in January 1863, the slaves in Texas were not notified until June 19, 1865. Thus, by law these slaves were free, but because they did not know or apply the truth of their freedom, they continued to function as slaves for two and a half additional years. Similarly, many people today have been set free through the empowering truth of God's Word, but because they have not internalized or actualized that freedom, they continue to live in bondage to sin and Satan's oppression.

One of the reasons believers often live as hostages to addictions or in spiritual bondage is because they either don't know the truth or don't embrace the truth they know. It is when you embrace, apply, and live out the truth that you are truly free. Jesus said you are to "know the truth, and the truth will make you free" (John 8:32). Those who are free no longer need to wear spiritual chains—a yoke of slavery, giving the illusion of freedom but not the truth of freedom in reality.

Unleashing God's rule in your life comes through a surrender and abandonment to the truth. It comes through overcoming your soul's temper tantrums when it hears the truth it doesn't want to hear. It comes through bringing your soul into alignment under the rule of God by using the Word of God as a mirror to reflect where you are right and where you are wrong in comparison to God's truth. When you reflect the truth of God through all you think, say, and do, you will not have to work hard to release His kingdom favor and benefits to you. God will do the work. Philippians 2:13

reminds us of this: "For it is God who is at work in you, both to will and to work for His good pleasure."

There is a common phrase today I hear when speaking or meeting with business-minded people or entrepreneurs: "Work smarter, not harder." In this chapter, I've given you the key to working smarter, not harder. Aligning your life with God's truth turns the work over to God Himself. After all, it is God who works in you and through you while you rest in an abiding relationship with His Son, Jesus Christ.

Let God do the work of unleashing His great pleasure throughout your life. When you do that, you'll come to know Him like never before. You'll witness His powerful hand move, maneuver, and maximize all that you do for your good, for the greater good of others, and for His glory and the expansion of His kingdom.

Chapter Seven

CREATING STRONG CONNECTIONS

Kingdom Provision

ONE DAY AN ATHEIST WAS WALKING THROUGH THE WOODS, admiring the beauty surrounding him. He gazed at the greatness of the trees. He listened to the melodies sung by the birds. He felt the flow of the breeze. Seeing the various creatures out and about as well as the foliage all around him, he felt uplifted. Yet, as he walked, he began to hear unusually loud rustling sounds behind him. Turning toward the sounds as they grew louder, he saw a seven-foot grizzly bear coming toward him. The man quickly took off running, terrified by the bear, but, as bears will do, the bear caught up with him.

The man fell in his haste and cried out to God. When he did, everything paused. The wind stopped blowing. The birds stopped singing. The animals stopped moving. And a voice came down from above, "Am I to take it now that you believe in Me?"

The man replied, "I don't want to be a hypocrite. I admit I've never believed in You and I can't really say I believe in You now, either, but I'm in trouble. So if you are real, could you please make this a Christian bear? I'll be satisfied with that."

Once the man spoke his request, the breeze began to blow again. The birds began to sing again. And the bear clasped his paws together and prayed, "For this food I am about to eat, I give You thanks."

This is obviously a fictional story told simply for humorous reasons. But it also has a point. It's a good reminder that it's easy to call on God when we are in trouble. It's easy to appeal to Him when life goes left. Many believers naturally look to Him as an escape valve or an escape hatch, all the while never recognizing Him for who He truly is in their everyday existence of life. Calling on God when you need a bailout but forgetting Him after you've been bailed out seems to be a regular occurrence for many believers today.

GOD AS THE ULTIMATE SOURCE

One of the primary themes surfacing in our time together in this book is God's preeminence. You are to seek first His kingdom. You are to prioritize His perspective. You are to make His will your primary goal. God is to be more to you than your Creator. He is to be recognized as your Lord, Father, Teacher, and Source. When we look to God as our Source, we look to Him as the supplier of all we have had, all we have, and all we will have. We also look to Him as the owner of all. This mental grid helps inform our decisions, but it also helps regulate our emotions. If you don't understand God as your Source and what that truly means for your life, your whole philosophy of life will be off. It will be skewed.

Time and time again in Scripture, God affirms His role as our Source:

> The earth is the Lord's, and all it contains,
> the world, and those who dwell in it.
> (Psalm 24:1)

> "For every beast of the forest is Mine,
> the cattle on a thousand hills.
> I know every bird of the mountains,
> and everything that moves in the field
> is Mine.
> If I were hungry I would not tell you,
> for the world is Mine, and all it contains."
> (Psalm 50:10–12)

O Lord, how many are Your works!
In wisdom You have made them all;
the earth is full of Your possessions.
(Psalm 104:24)

"The silver is Mine and the gold is Mine,"
declares the Lord of hosts. (Haggai 2:8)

"Worthy are You, our Lord and our God,
to receive glory and honor and power;
for You created all things, and because
of Your will they existed, and were
created." (Revelation 4:11)

God wants us to get one thing straight: He made it all. He owns it all. Everything in creation belongs to Him. If and when you do not start there philosophically, you seek to usurp God's role in your life. When you do that, you will place yourself in conflict with the true owner. There's only one owner and that is God.

If you'll remember the house-sitting illustration I shared with you in the previous chapter, I want you to consider what would have happened if I started acting as if I owned the house. Imagine if the owners returned and I refused to leave. You can bet if I stayed persistent on remaining there, the owners would have called the cops or a counselor to get me booted out. Similarly, difficult consequences will occur when you or I seek to think or act as if we own God's creation and all He has given to us. But God is the owner. He is our Source.

As the owner, God does allow us to manage His resources. We call this stewardship. We are called and equipped to steward the time, talents, and treasures God places within our sphere of responsibility. What often happens, though, is we confuse the resource with the Source. But the resources are merely the vehicles through which you receive what you need.

For example, when you go grocery shopping, you realize the grocery store is not your source of food. The grocery store is a resource to distribute to you what you eat. If the grocery store was the source, that would mean it was not dependent upon something else to supply you with food. We all know the grocery store is dependent upon suppliers to provide us with what we need.

Confusing a resource with the Source causes all sorts of trouble. Understanding that God is your Source allows you to think outside the box of the various resources or mechanisms He uses to supply you with what you need. It frees your emotions so you do not have to worry about whether your resources will be stocked or in supply, because you know that God supplies your every need.

When King David set out to build the temple, he faced a gargantuan task. Here was this former shepherd boy coordinating a massive building project requiring thousands of workers and more money than his young mind could have ever fathomed. And yet David was perfect for the job because his heart knew God as his Source. He had witnessed God enable him to defeat the giant Goliath. He had witnessed God protect him from Saul's attacks. He had seen how God supplied all of his needs throughout his life, so the idea of building a temple—when viewed through the lens of God as his Source—was an idea he could understand. We know that David saw God as his Source because of the prayer and instructions recorded for us in 1 Chronicles 29. The passage I want to look at contains eleven verses, but it's worth reading in its entirety so that we can identify the many ways David recognized God as his Source.

> So David blessed the Lord in the sight of all the assembly; and David said, "Blessed are You, O Lord God of Israel our father, forever and ever. Yours, O Lord, is the greatness and the power and the glory and the victory and the majesty, indeed everything that is in the heavens and the earth; Yours is the dominion, O Lord, and You exalt Yourself as head over all. Both riches and honor come from You, and You rule over all, and in Your hand is power and might; and it lies in Your hand to make great and to strengthen everyone. Now therefore, our God, we thank You, and praise Your glorious name.
>
> "But who am I and who are my people that we should be able to offer as generously as this? For all things come from You, and from Your hand we have given You. For we are sojourners before You, and tenants, as all our fathers were; our days on the earth are like a shadow, and there is no hope. O Lord our God, all this abundance that we have provided to build You a house for Your holy name, it is from Your hand, and all is Yours. Since I know, O my God, that You try the heart and delight in uprightness, I, in the integrity of my heart, have willingly offered all these

things; so now with joy I have seen Your people, who are present here, make their offerings willingly to You.

"O Lord, the God of Abraham, Isaac and Israel, our fathers, preserve this forever in the intentions of the heart of Your people, and direct their heart to You; and give to my son Solomon a perfect heart to keep Your commandments, Your testimonies and Your statutes, and to do them all, and to build the temple, for which I have made provision."

Then David said to all the assembly, "Now bless the Lord your God." And all the assembly blessed the Lord, the God of their fathers, and bowed low and did homage to the Lord and to the king. (1 Chronicles 29:10–20)

Repeatedly in this prayer David emphasized God as his Source. He recognized that all things come from God. In fact, in verse 14 he let it be known that even whatever he or the people offered to God actually came from God to begin with.

This reminds me of an experience I had with one of my kids. It was coming up on my birthday, they asked me for money so they could buy me a gift. Maybe that's happened to you, too, and you can understand how that makes you feel, especially when you receive the gift that you paid for. And even more especially if you don't like the gift they picked out, again a gift that you paid for.

David understood that even the gifts and offerings they gave to God came from God. In that sense, he was encouraging himself and the others to remain mindful of what they offered God. After all, if God is the supplier of their gifts to Him, what they give Him should be something He wants. As well, what they give Him should come with a heart of gratitude for having been given the ability to give it at all.

A HEART OF GRATITUDE

How often do you consider that what you give to God (your time, talents, or treasures) actually originated from God? I imagine it would make a difference in what you offer were you to make that much more of a consideration in your everyday life. God is the owner of all we have. Even the tithe we give comes from Him. Even the time we give comes from Him. Even the talents we give come from Him. To give generously back to the One who has given to you evokes a heart of gratitude in the process, rather than a heart of pride or entitlement.

Yet far too often we view our time, talents, and treasures through a lens of entitlement. We assume we deserve whatever it is we have. This can then produce a heart of resentment, blame, or even bitterness toward God when what we have is removed from us. Yet when we realize that all things are a gift given by God to be used, enjoyed, or maximized for a time, we hold what we have in our hands more loosely. We honor what we have in our hearts more gratefully. When we truly understand James 1:17—"Every good thing given and every perfect gift is from above, coming down from the Father of lights, with whom there is no variation or shifting

When we realize that all things are a gift given by God to be used, enjoyed, or maximized for a time, we hold what we have in our hands more loosely. We honor what we have in our hearts more gratefully.

shadow"—it causes us to live out the fullness of God's calling to be a "cheerful giver" (2 Corinthians 9:7).

Identifying God as your Source shifts your perspective, which then strengthens your emotions. It means you no longer have to lose your mind when your resources don't look to be working out. Or if the bank turns you down for whatever it is you were needing, you don't need to worry. God supplies "all your needs" when you make His purpose your purpose (Philippians 4:19).

I'll never forget learning this lesson early in my ministry. I had been pastoring a small church of fewer than a hundred people for a number of years. We had started out meeting in my home but then moved on to meet at various places, like school buildings or an apartment community activity room. But over time we were finding it increasingly more difficult to rent, set up each Sunday, and take everything down immediately afterward. We knew we needed our own building. The problem was that no bank would loan us the money. We didn't have enough credit or equity to make a strong case for them to do so.

Thus, when we found a small A-frame building for sale not more than a stone's throw from where I lived with my family at that time, we went to God to ask for the money to buy it. Our members couldn't contribute enough to cover the price. But we continued to put the building and its cost before the Lord in prayer. Then one day I was meeting with a businessman in Dallas about another matter, and he began to ask me about our search for a permanent church home. When I told him about the A-frame building we had found and the money we needed to purchase it, another man overheard our conversation. He peeked his head into the room where we were meeting and asked to join our discussion. At first I was put off and annoyed by his interruption. But that quickly passed when he pulled out his checkbook to write me a check for the amount we needed to purchase the A-frame building.

Keep in mind, I had never met this man before in my life. If I had spent my time strategizing who to talk to in order to raise the funds to purchase the A-frame building, this man's name would not have made it on my list. But thankfully my list of who to talk to about raising the funds actually started with the most important name of all: God. And because God knew my need and that I had placed my need in His hands to accomplish a kingdom purpose, He connected me with a resource to supply that need not only easily but also quickly.

Stewarding your resources well in light of recognizing God as your Source is a kingdom issue. It involves exercising the dominion God has placed in your jurisdiction of personal and corporate responsibility. Just as David was tasked with stewarding the development of the temple, you have been assigned certain tasks for developing that which falls under your influence. As you learn how best to see God as your Source and to rely on Him, you'll discover the unleashing of His provision to you. God always supplies that which He calls you to do. The problems come when you look outside of God to supply the things He has put on your heart to do.

If you are familiar with Aesop's fables, you'll know about the goose that laid golden eggs. Every day the goose would lay a new golden egg. Unfortunately the people opted to kill the goose because they thought they could collect all the golden eggs inside the goose. But when they killed the goose, there were no eggs inside her. They learned that only the living goose could produce a golden egg. Unfortunately, we have a generation of people today who are looking for ways to produce their own golden eggs. As a result, they are seeking to rid themselves of God so they can produce what they want when they want it. They do this without realizing that God is the Source. There's no getting rid of God in this equation, at least not with any positive outcome.

The blessings of financial provision that flow from heaven to you come from God. He is your Source. As David prayed, God is "the greatness and the power and the glory and the victory and the majesty, indeed everything that is in the heavens and the earth; Yours is the dominion, O Lord, and You exalt Yourself as head over all. Both riches and honor come from You, and You rule over all, and in Your hand is power and might; and it lies in Your hand to make great and to strengthen everyone" (1 Chronicles 29:11–12).

When you realize this as truth, you will respond as David did in the very next verse: "Now therefore, our God, we thank You, and praise Your glorious name" (v. 13). Giving God thanks reveals a heart that recognizes His position as your provider. Giving God praise acknowledges His sovereign wisdom in His provision. God knows what you need and when you need it even more than you do (Matthew

6:32). You may think you know best, but God always knows best. He sees the end from the beginning and all of the pieces in between.

You live in God's home. If you want your own home, then you need to go out and create your own planet and universe to support it. But until that happens, you'll need to recognize that God is the owner over this one.

Have you ever had a teenager living in your home who forgot you were their provider? They may argue for their independence so they can come in at any hour of the night, but since you are the one paying the mortgage, electricity, and more, you have the right to set the time when they come home. Similarly, you live in God's home. If you want your own home, then you need to go out and create your own planet and universe to support it. But until that happens, you'll need to recognize that God is the owner over this one. His rules reign supreme. How you use the resources He's given you (including your time and your talents) is up to Him. Should you choose to use them differently or for selfish gain, you'll face the consequences just as your teenager would face the consequences for breaking curfew and coming in late.

There must exist a kingdom mindset for operating from the realm of divine rule. Your mentality must inform your decisions in a way that puts God's perspective first. God doesn't want you coming to Him with your needs after you have exhausted all other avenues. God wants you and me to come to Him first. He wants us to honor Him first. We are mere beneficiaries of God's great grace and provision. We are to maximize that which He gives us for the greater good of all as well as for the advancement of God's own glory and kingdom.

THE TEMPLE AS A KINGDOM REPRESENTATION

The context of David's prayer acknowledging God as the Source for all he had was during the preparations for the building of the temple. The Israelites were moving from a mobile temple, which was called the tabernacle, and looking to erect a permanent building—the temple. The temple was designed to do three things: provide spiritual guidance for the nation of Israel, provide an environment for the care and well-being of the people, and influence the culture. In fact, Moses had declared many years before that when the culture around them saw how wise their God was and how the followers of God functioned and operated, they would fear God as they should and honor Him (Deuteronomy 4:5–8).

In Ezekiel we read about how life comes down from the altar and into the aisles of the temple and then flows out the door into the streets and the world (47:1–12). This provides a visual illustration of how the temple was to influence the local people and those beyond the immediate region. The temple, much like the church today, was to have a positive kingdom impact on the known world. In fact, both the Old and the New Testaments refer to this temple as "God's house" or

"God's household." We see this comparison to the church in the New Testament in Ephesians 2:

> And He came and preached peace to you who were far away, and peace to those who were near; for through Him we both have our access in one Spirit to the Father. So then you are no longer strangers and aliens, but you are fellow citizens with the saints, and are of God's household, having been built on the foundation of the apostles and prophets, Christ Jesus Himself being the corner stone, in whom the whole building, being fitted together, is growing into a holy temple in the Lord, in whom you also are being built together into a dwelling of God in the Spirit. (vv. 17–22)

And while God exists in infinitude, making it impossible for any house to truly hold God within, His house exists as a localized representation of His presence in history. It's where His shekinah glory manifests itself visibly and spreads out into the community and the world. First Timothy 3:15 describes the house of God: "The household of God, which is the church of the living God, the pillar and support of the truth." The temple and the church are to function as pillars of truth.

We looked at the purpose and importance of truth in the previous chapter, so I won't go into that again, but I want to emphasize that the advancement of God's kingdom program on earth flows out from His house—the church. What's more, it flows out when members of His body function in oneness and unity together, aligned under His rule and looking to Him as the ultimate and only Source. The collective church body could be so much more effective at influencing our culture for good if we would understand and apply this reality to our lives. Yet far too often people show up at worship selfish, *not* worship service. They come only to get their latest blessing or their current word-for-the-week to guide them along life's journey. But for the church to collectively unleash God's kingdom impact on culture, we need to serve Him and serve others under His overarching rule.

AVOIDING THE PERILS OF FORGETTING GOD

One of the reasons we've lost our cultural influence is because the church has decided it wants to be more cultural than Christian. It wants to please society rather than please the Source. It wants to function based on secular thinking rather than spiritual wisdom, being more tied to the kingdoms of this world order than to the kingdom of our God and Christ, our Lord. Only when we return to a right relationship with God and with each other will we tap into and unleash our kingdom influence in social structures and the world. We do this when we decide to take God seriously, no longer marginalizing Him outside of the confines of our individual and collective focus.

Deuteronomy 8 warns us of what can come about when we forget to take God seriously. It reveals to us what can happen when we begin to look to the resources of our lives as the source.

> "Beware that you do not forget the Lord your God by not keeping His commandments and His ordinances and His statutes which I am commanding you today; otherwise, when you have eaten and are satisfied, and have built good houses and lived in them, and when your herds and your flocks multiply, and your silver and gold multiply, and all that you have multiplies, then your heart will become proud and you will forget the Lord your God who brought you out from the land of Egypt, out of the house of slavery. He led you through the great and terrible wilderness, with its fiery serpents and scorpions and thirsty ground where there was no water; He brought water for you out of the rock of flint. In the wilderness He fed you manna which your fathers did not know, that He might humble you and that He might test you, to do good for you in the end. Otherwise, you may say in your heart, 'My power and the strength of my hand made me this wealth.' But you shall remember the Lord your God, for it is He who is giving you power to make wealth, that He may confirm His covenant which He swore to your fathers, as it is this day." (vv. 11–18)

You and I must put God first. We are to remember God in all we do because it is God who unleashes the power to make wealth and to provide all we need to carry out His will on earth. We cannot forget Him in the good times. We cannot forget Him when we feel life is under our control. David had amassed a large sum of money for the building of the temple. You would think that it would have been easy to forget his need for God during this prosperous time, but David reminded us why God called him a "man after His own heart" (1 Samuel 13:14), because in David's prosperity, he reminded himself, others, and also God that he knew who the Source truly was.

HONORING GOD IN ABUNDANCE AND SCARCITY

God doesn't oppose your prospering or developing your resources. He just wants to be sure you remember Him when you do. He wants you to remember that He can shut it all down in a heartbeat should you forget who is your true Source. God provides the life you live. God gives you the breath you breathe. God enables you to move with strength. It only takes a season of ill health or chronic pain to remind you of what matters most. Without these things, your wealth does nothing for you anyhow. That's why it's important to honor God in all you do, but especially when He's blessed you abundantly.

When you honor Him in the lean times and in the times of blessing, He honors you with His covering and His provisional care.

I remember when Lois and I had a monthly income of only $350 to live on. Despite the difficulties of raising a family on this small income, we always gave God the first $50 we received each month. We gave $35 to go toward the tithe and then we gave $15 over and above the tithe. We did that every month regardless of what else we may have needed. Without fail we always had what we needed. God was our Source, and He remains my Source today. When you honor Him in the lean times and in the times of blessing, He honors you with His covering and His provisional care. That provision may come through unexpected ways, but you can count on God to meet your needs when you steward all that He has given you with the intention and action of honoring Him (Proverbs 3:9–10).

Unleashing the provision of God in your life starts with recognizing Him as the sole provider of all you need. It requires a mindset shift as you understand that His hand supplies all. Have you heard the phrase, often associated with dogs, "Don't bite the hand that feeds you"? It doesn't apply only to dogs. God is our ultimate Source in all things. We would be wise not to bite the hand that feeds us but rather to show gratitude, honor, and allegiance to Him instead.

Chapter Eight

REVEALING HIDDEN INSIGHTS

Kingdom Mysteries

EVERYONE LOVES A GOOD MYSTERY. A WHODUNIT ALWAYS gives the mind a moment to focus on details, figure out nuances, read between the lines, and try to outsmart the next person by solving the mystery first. In the Bible, mystery refers to something hidden in the Old Testament that is later explained in the New Testament. It's something unclear, like a shadow, that becomes clear in time. A biblical mystery often conceals the principle until it's time for it to be revealed. That's why the Old Testament is full of symbols and analogies. These situations set up the New Testament fulfillment, or revelation.

A lot of Jesus' ministry was about revealing the meaning of the Old Testament mysteries. He spoke wisdom and clarity into the minds of His listeners, oftentimes through parables. A parable is a story that illustrates a moral or spiritual truth. Not everyone can understand the meaning of a parable. There must be a heart to understand and the ability to discern spiritual or moral truths.

One particular parable is found in Luke 8, where Jesus talked about seed sown in a variety of ways. Following the telling of the parable, the disciples asked Jesus to explain its meaning to them. They were unable to figure it out themselves. That's when Jesus referenced the mysterious nature of this parable. We read this in Luke 8:9–10: "His disciples began questioning Him as to what this parable meant. And He said, 'To you it has been granted to know the mysteries of the kingdom of God, but to the rest it is in parables, so that seeing they may not see, and hearing they may not understand.'" The kingdom of God is a mystery. No one can fully understand the insights and the wisdom within it. Any understanding comes from the Spirit; it is a gift often wrapped in the context of a contemporary reality.

Jesus was a master storyteller, taking truth and translating it into a language people could make sense of and then apply in their everyday lives. One way He did this was through identifying a cognitive experience and turning it into an analogous spiritual revelation. This then offered those who had been granted the gift of spiritual insight the ability to understand the mystery while shrouding it from those who did not have ears to hear. You might consider it in modern terms as speaking in code.

The reason why parables were often given as a way to reveal truth to a limited number of people was because Jesus knew who His true followers were. He also knew those who only wanted to follow Him for the goods and the miracles He could provide. Jesus wasn't interested in revealing His mysteries to opportunists. He sought out true kingdom disciples in whom to plant the seeds of spiritual wisdom.

Jesus wasn't interested in revealing His mysteries to opportunists. He sought out true kingdom disciples in whom to plant the seeds of spiritual wisdom.

THE SEED AND THE SOIL

Let's start by looking at the parable of the sower:

> When a large crowd was coming together, and those from the various cities were journeying to Him, He spoke by way of a parable: "The sower went out to sow his seed;

> and as he sowed, some fell beside the road, and it was trampled under foot and the birds of the air ate it up. Other seed fell on rocky soil, and as soon as it grew up, it withered away, because it had no moisture. Other seed fell among the thorns; and the thorns grew up with it and choked it out. Other seed fell into the good soil, and grew up, and produced a crop a hundred times as great." As He said these things, He would call out, "He who has ears to hear, let him hear." (Luke 8:4–8)

The parable itself involves a farmer. In biblical days, they did not have the technology and tractors that we have today. Yet they were still largely an agrarian culture. Thus, what they would often do is strap a bag onto the back of a donkey. This bag would have seed in it. The farmer would walk alongside the donkey with a pouch on his head as well. As needed, the farmer transferred the seed from the large bag on the donkey to the smaller pouch on his own head. Then he would scatter the seed in the various locations. That way he did not run out of seed quickly and could cover the most ground efficiently.

In this parable, we learn about a farmer who sows seed beside the road, on rocky soil, in thorny areas, and then also in good soil. Perhaps he was testing the quality of his seed, because that doesn't sound like a normal farming approach. But, regardless, we also learn that where the seed landed had a lot to do with the quality and quantity of the crop.

The seed beside the road produced no crop at all; the birds ate it up before it could grow. The seed on the rocky soil also produced no crop, because as soon as the sprouts grew, they withered due to a lack of moisture. The seed that fell among the thorns likewise produced no crop, because the thorns and weeds choked out the sprouts. Only the seed in the good soil produced a crop. In fact, this seed produced a crop a hundred times as great as the others. It would require only one test by any farmer to know where to plant his next batch of seed—in the good soil. Wasting his time and his seed in the other soil would be foolish.

It's fairly easy to understand the story, even if you aren't a farmer yourself. The surface-level truth of this parable wouldn't leave too many people scratching their heads: Plant your seed in good soil if you want your crop to grow. It's pretty simple and straightforward.

But the disciples knew Jesus wasn't offering a master class in farming. He was disclosing spiritual truth. That's why they asked Him for a deeper explanation of what it meant. Jesus began His explanation in verse 11 by telling what the seed symbolized: "Now the parable is this: the seed is the word of God." Thus, in every reference to the seed in His story, Jesus meant the Word of God. Essentially, you can substitute "the Word of God" in the story and it would look like this:

> "The sower went out to sow [the Word of God]; and as he sowed, some fell beside the road, and it was trampled under foot and the birds of the air ate it up. Other [words of God] fell on rocky soil, and as soon as it grew up, it withered away, because it had no moisture. Other [words of God] fell among the thorns; and the thorns grew up

> with it and choked it out. Other [words of God] fell into the good soil, and grew up, and produced a crop a hundred times as great."

Sometimes it helps to insert the meaning directly into the parable. We can see that the Word of God landed in different places, and the places upon which it landed affected whether the Word of God produced anything at all. This reveals to us first and foremost that it is not the power of the Word of God that determined what happened. Rather, it was the condition of the soil. Just like the seed the farmer planted, the Word of God can produce great things. Intrinsic in it is all that is needed to produce a bumper crop of spiritual life and growth. So if ever the Word of God does not grow, it's not a problem with the Bible. It's a soil issue. It's because the soil in which the Word of God fell is deficient.

THE WORD OF GOD AND ITS POWER

Whenever the Word of God is not working in your life, you can gather from this parable that you are not to blame the seed. You are not to blame the Bible. The Bible is a living document, always able to produce great growth. The determiner of that growth is the ground in which it is received. Hebrews 4 tells us,

> For the word of God is living and active and sharper than any two-edged sword, and piercing as far as the division

> of soul and spirit, of both joints and marrow, and able to judge the thoughts and intentions of the heart. And there is no creature hidden from His sight, but all things are open and laid bare to the eyes of Him with whom we have to do. (vv. 12–13)

The Word of God always works. It always pierces. It always produces life. But if it falls on errant soil, such as a faulty heart, it won't do what the Word of God is designed to do. Not because it's incapable, but because in the environment in which God's Word finds itself it is unable to take root or thrive.

No doubt Jesus chose the term *seed* in this parable because it provides an easily understandable illustration of a spiritual truth. But this isn't the only time seed is spoken of in Scripture. In fact, in the first chapter of 1 Peter we read about imperishable seed, which is the Word of God.

> Since you have in obedience to the truth purified your souls for a sincere love of the brethren, fervently love one another from the heart, for you have been born again not of seed which is perishable but imperishable, that is, through the living and enduring word of God. For,
>
> > "All flesh is like grass,
> > And all its glory like the flower of grass.
> > The grass withers,
> > And the flower falls off,
> > But the word of the Lord endures forever."

The Word of God always works. It always pierces. It always produces life. But if it falls on errant soil, such as a faulty heart, it won't do what the Word of God is designed to do.

> And this is the word which was preached to you. (vv. 22–25)

The seed is the life-giving force in order to birth a new reality. It's designed to penetrate the soil of the heart and spirit in order to produce a new life of spiritual maturity. But just as sperm fails to enter an egg and thus life does not form, the seed of the Word of God must also be able to penetrate the soil of our spirit to produce its new life.

BODY, SOUL, AND SPIRIT

To better understand this, we need to look at the way we've been designed by God. First Thessalonians 5:23 says that we are composed of body, soul, and spirit. All of us have these three cognates composed to create our humanity. First, your body gives you the ability to function in the physical world through your five senses. It includes your ability to communicate and interact with the world. Second, your soul is your personhood. It's who you are. You are not your body. Your body is a suit for your soul. Your soul is your real essence. That's why, when a person dies, the soul leaves the body and the body decays. The soul allows you to communicate with yourself. Third, your spirit is your relational entity placed inside you to communicate with God.

The problem is that we were all born with a deadened spirit due to sin. Ephesians 2:1 says, "And you were dead in your trespasses and sins." Each of us comes into this world spiritually dead and unable to communicate with God. As a result of this severing in relational communication, our souls have a defect as well. That's why a parent never has to teach a child to lie. A parent doesn't have to teach a child to be selfish. The soul we are born with has been tainted by sin and understands the nature of sin.

As we grow and develop, if we remain separated from God in our spirit, then our soul continues to become corrupted. This shows up at differing levels for different people, but without God we are all messed up somehow. The worse our soul gets, the more errant activity the body participates in. This is because the body obeys the soul. The soul is your mind, emotions, will, and consciousness. The soul interjects its desires, wants, and needs into the body.

A crazy-acting person is really just a crazy soul displaying itself through the form of a body. That's why trying to fix the body by addressing the body only produces temporary gains. The way to fix the body and what the body does is by addressing the soul. But the only part of us able to truly heal the soul is our spirit. Our communion with God informs our communion with ourselves in our mind, emotions, will, and consciousness. But because the spirit is dead and the soul is defective, the body often carries the greatest influence on what we do. This happens when we give in to our passions, laziness, or any number of things.

The solution comes through salvation. When a person is converted to Jesus Christ, believing in Him for the gift of eternal life and the forgiveness of sin, accepting Him as their personal sin bearer, the living seed of God penetrates that person's spirit. This penetration creates a new life. Second Corinthians 5:17 puts it this way: "Therefore if anyone is in Christ, he is a new creature; the old things passed away; behold, new things have come."

This quickening of the spirit produces a conception of new life. Keep in mind, this conception can be compared to a fertilized egg. It does not express the full maturity contained within it. It is life, but it must grow and develop in order to function at its highest capacity. This growth is often what we refer to as spiritual maturity. The ability of this growth, though, relies on several factors. Just as a baby in the womb needs nourishment to develop, the spirit needs the right nourishment to develop as well. Just as a baby in the womb needs the right environment in which to develop, the spirit needs the right environment in which to develop as well.

The living spirit left unattended will not grow on its own. It must have the seed of the Word of God (the nourishment) to grow. Not only that, it must have the right environment (the good soil) to grow as well. The condition of the soul and its receptivity to the Word of God will determine the expansion of new life into maturity. Both will determine how much of God's will, power, and favor you unleash in your life.

BARRIERS TO SPIRITUAL GROWTH

Jesus' parable of the sower helps us to identify different ways Satan seeks to keep believers from maturing spiritually. The first way involves seed that falls along the roadside. When the seed is left vulnerable along the road, birds come by to pick it up or people trample on it. In other words, returning to the baby-in-the-womb example, seed that falls along the road doesn't allow the sperm to reach the egg. It's not that the Word of God isn't heard. The Word of God is there. Just like sperm is present after marital intimacy even when it doesn't penetrate an egg. But the Word of God doesn't penetrate beyond the surface level of the ear. It's just information in one ear and out the other. And because it doesn't penetrate beneath the surface, Satan is able to send demons and people to either snatch it or trample it. In that way, the Word of God never reaches the spirit within.

The next illustration Jesus gave us in this parable involves the seed that fell on rocky soil. In this situation we see that those who heard the Word of God actually received it. In fact, they received it with joy. But because they did not have a firm root or the soil to allow for the embedding and developing of a firm root, they only believed the Word for a while. Then when temptations came, they fell away (Luke 8:13).

This second example may remind you of people who say amen and are temporarily active in church, but as soon as a problem shows up or a difficulty arises, they fall away. They forget that God is good all the time and all the time God is good. These statements become mere platitudes for them when convenient. Because they did not allow the Word of God to get rooted within them, the winds and troubles of this life arise and choke out any life that had grown above the surface.

Many individuals in the current "deconstruction" trend culturally fall into this category. They wanted spiritual truth when it suited them, but they stopped going to church or believing in spiritual truths when things got tough. Without an initial depth of discovery for themselves, their spirituality was really just someone else's religion. Should that someone else let them down or disappoint them, they throw the whole thing out.

I would argue that many, if not most, who are deconstructing their Christianity never truly knew Christ personally for themselves. Or if they did, they knew of Him more than abided in and with Him. I say this because Jesus cannot disappoint. Isaiah 49:23 puts it like this: "Kings will be your foster fathers, and their queens your nursing mothers. They will bow down before you with their faces to the ground; they will lick the dust at your feet. Then you will know that I am the Lord; those who hope in me will not be disappointed" (NIV)

The third example from the parable includes the seed that fell among thorns. This refers to those who not only hear the Word but even aim to apply it. They work at their spiritual growth in the ways they can. The problems show up when the worries, riches, or even pleasures of this life choke out any spiritual life the Word produces. What they wind up with is stunted spiritual growth, not full spiritual development. They have stalks with no fruit or flowers. The things that Satan can use to choke out the Word in these believers don't have to be bad. He can choke out their spiritual growth with wealth or worldliness. Anytime the physical world becomes more important than the spiritual world and is prioritized in thoughts and actions, it chokes out the work of the Word of

God. The spiritual life is not allowed to have its way because it gets strangled by wealth and the world's values.

Keep in mind there's nothing wrong with wealth. The problem tied to wealth is when wealth becomes more important than the kingdom values given to us by God. Wealth becomes a detriment when it feeds worldliness. Worldliness has to do with everything plugging into a central concept revolving around society's order and values that leave God out. Just like you have the world of sports, the world of finance, or the world of politics, what the term *world* means in those instances is a devotion and dedication to that which it defines. Thus, worldliness elevates the world's ways to the exclusion of God's ways. It elevates the secular over the sacred.

Not too long ago I did a Bible study teaching in Las Vegas. You might think that's an odd place to film a Bible study, but when I tell you the topic of the study was the seven churches in Revelation, it makes more sense. Yet as I was doing the Bible study taping amid the opulence of that city, it dawned on me how very difficult it would be to live as a strong Christian there. It certainly wouldn't be impossible, and I'm sure there are many strong Christians who live in the Vegas area, but there are also things that could make it challenging. I saw many ways for spiritual development and nourishment to get choked out. There's money, narcissism, clothes, pleasure, entertainment, and a myriad of other things Satan would love to use to strangle the spiritual life of any believer. It would be a greater challenge to grow the Word of God within you there.

The very last session that I filmed in Vegas was done at a

famous wedding chapel. It's where a lot of celebrities have been married. I was teaching the session on "returning to your first love" from the second chapter of Revelation. While I was taping, the owner of the chapel told us the story about a celebrity who was married there one evening only to get divorced the next morning. Needless to say, this person was so inebriated from partying all night long that the decision to get married was an impulse. It's just one more example of how the world and its ways can choke out any sense a person may have.

For you to unleash the kingdom of God and His Word in your life, you need to be cautious around things that lead to worldliness. You need to put up blinders against the things that tempt you to live a worldly life according to the values of pleasure or hedonism. The world's soil will suck the spiritual life out of anyone, causing you to be a stunted Christian. But remember, this isn't because there's a defect with the Word of God. No, the Word of God is perfect. The defect is in the soil itself.

BEARING FRUIT THROUGH SPIRITUAL ALIGNMENT

The only soil that produces growth in Jesus' parable was the good soil. He explained what that good soil meant to His disciples: "But the seed in the good soil, these are the ones who have heard the word in an honest and good heart, and hold it fast, and bear fruit with perseverance" (Luke 8:15). The good soil includes an honest and good heart. This starts by being honest with God. You have to willingly acknowledge where you and the Word of God disagree. You can't be a yes-man or a yes-woman to God, agreeing outwardly but disagreeing inwardly. Honesty is the primary ingredient in good soil.

Yet not only do you need to be honest with God, but you also need to be honest with yourself. You have to willingly acknowledge where you have fallen short or where you continue to fall short. You have to surrender your honest desires if and when they disagree with God's Word. You need to get real and raw with the Lord. He knows the truth anyhow. You might as well admit to Him how you feel, where you struggle, and in what ways you need His help the most.

You can't be a yes-man or a yes-woman to God, agreeing outwardly but disagreeing inwardly. Honesty is the primary ingredient in good soil.

In addition to honesty and goodness, though, you also need to hold fast to the Word of God. In other words, don't just hear it and forget it. Don't leave it sitting in the pew as you head out of church. Holding fast to the Word of God means to hold tight. Meditate on it. Nurture it in you. As James states: "My dear brothers and sisters, take note of this: Everyone should be quick to listen, slow to speak and slow to become angry, because human anger does not produce the righteousness that God desires. Therefore, get rid of all moral filth and the evil that is so prevalent and humbly accept the word planted in you, which can save you" (1:19–21 NIV).

To receive the Word in you means to "humbly accept" the Word of God. In this way the Word of God is able to save your soul by transforming your soul. There are two types of salvation in Scripture relating to our life on earth. One is the salvation we receive when we trust in Christ for the forgiveness of our sins. That is eternal salvation. But the saving James referred to in this passage is an ongoing sanctification of your soul. It's a growth reality.

When I toured Corinth recently and went through the excellent museum they have at the archeological site, I saw some mirrors from the days of the New Testament. At first I didn't recognize the mirrors as mirrors. They looked like the bottom of a pot. But that's because in biblical days glass mirrors didn't exist. The way people saw themselves back then was with a brass mirror, which required them to adjust the brass in just the right way so they could see their reflection. It was a complicated process of manipulating the brass or its position relative to the sun or a candle to get the right reflection. When James told us we are to receive the Word implanted and to hold fast to it, he referred to this example of a mirror in the next few verses:

> But prove yourselves doers of the word, and not merely hearers who delude themselves. For if anyone is a hearer of the word and not a doer, he is like a man who looks at his natural face in a mirror; for once he has looked at himself and gone away, he has immediately forgotten what kind of person he was. But one who looks intently at the perfect law, the law of liberty, and abides by it, not having

> become a forgetful hearer but an effectual doer, this man will be blessed in what he does. (vv. 22–25)

James was encouraging his readers to look intently at God's Word until they saw their face in it. Similarly we are to examine the Word on such a level that we stare at it and allow the reflection to show us the image of God and His values made manifest in our lives. We are to allow the mirror of His Word to define us. Where we do not align with the mirror image, we need to adjust. In that manner, we will become more than a "forgetful hearer"; we will become an "effectual doer" of the Word of God (v. 25). In short, we will produce fruit that will last. John 15:16 speaks of this fruit: "You did not choose Me but I chose you, and appointed you that you would go and bear fruit, and that your fruit would remain, so that whatever you ask of the Father in My name He may give to you."

When you bear fruit that will last, you are in alignment with God and unleashing His will in your life. As the verse just revealed to us, you can "ask of the Father in [Jesus'] name" and He will give it to you. Talk about unleashing power. Talk about spiritual victory. Your ability to tap into the life you have been designed to live out comes through your allowing the Word of God to take root in your humble and good heart and meditating on it, staring at it. Then you apply the truth from the Word intentionally as you seek to mirror the image of God in all you do. It is then that you will produce the visible fruit from the seed planted within.

Fruit always has three characteristics. First, it always

bears the character of the tree of which it is a part, or the seed. You won't find oranges on apple trees. You won't find apples on pear trees. The character of the tree (the seed) determines the nature of the fruit.

Second, fruit is always visible. You've never seen invisible fruit. And I can guarantee you've never eaten invisible fruit either. Just like when a woman becomes pregnant and her body reveals the presence of the baby through the expansion of her size, fruit reveals the presence of the Holy Spirit in your life.

Third, fruit exists for the benefit of another. The only fruit that eats itself is rotten fruit. Your fruit as a believer in Jesus Christ is made to help others and advance God's kingdom agenda on earth. When you seek to hoard the blessings and benefits given to you by God, you become like rotten fruit that is consuming itself. Fruit always exists for the enjoyment and benefit of someone else.

It's critical to understand the parable of the sower in its full context. Jesus gave His disciples insight so they could mature and develop in their walk with Him. That insight has been preserved through the inspired Word of God so you and I can also learn how to mature and develop our walk with God and impact the lives of others. In doing so, we will become visible representatives of God's kingdom plan on earth, bringing good to others and glory to God.

Chapter Nine

LIVING IN ABUNDANCE

Kingdom Blessings

AROUND THE START OF THE TWENTY-FIRST CENTURY, A major blackout occurred on the East Coast. I happened to be there when it took place. Lois was traveling with me, and we made our way to the airport to head back home to Dallas. Everything about that day seemed normal. We stood in line at the airport, waiting with hundreds of others to board our flight, and then the blackout hit. As you might imagine, chaos ensued. Confusion set in. Thoughts went from concern for the moment to worry about the future. With no power, all flights were grounded. People's plans changed not only for that period of time but for the days ahead.

Not only did flights get canceled, but the train stations also shut down. In short, there was no way out of New York for anyone who didn't own a car. A massive power grid failure had occurred, and millions of people were in the grip of the unknown—Lois and me included. The power grid failure actually had taken place in Canada, but the effects could be felt all the way down the East Coast. We, along with others, waited at the airport for hours in hopes that, as it often does, the power would simply come back on. Eventually we were told to make our way to a hotel as they did not believe the power would be restored anytime soon.

Finding a hotel in New York City when the city has no power was a challenge. Finding a hotel in New York City with thousands of other stranded individuals made it even worse. I was thankful that my assistant in Dallas, Sylvia, could look for a room for us while we looked for a cab to take us back into the city. Sylvia managed to reserve the last available room at the Crown Plaza near the airport. When we arrived, the scene resembled something you might see in a movie. The eerily dark lobby welcomed us with a foreboding presence. We had to sign for our room with a flashlight and then make our way up the staircase, also with a flashlight, luggage in hand. Thankfully the room had a window, so we went to open the curtains and let some air in, as the room had become muggy and warm.

We were able to crack the window open enough to hear the soft sounds of music outside. In the silence of darkness, the music was a nice surprise, but we wondered where it came from. As we looked farther out the window, we could see a nearby hotel, the Marriott, all lit up. We instantly wondered how there could be so much light in the midst of so much darkness.

Thus, we decided to make our way back down the dark stairwell, out the front door into the blackness of night, and then across the street to the Marriott. What we found inside amazed us. Not only did they have music, but they also had hot food, televisions playing CNN in the foyer with ongoing news on the blackout, and people gathered around talking. It was a far different scene than we had witnessed at the airport or even at our own hotel. People were relaxed. The atmosphere was still a bit chaotic simply due to the challenges the city was facing at that time, but it was also inviting. In fact, smiles greeted those who walked in from outdoors.

I've always been naturally inquisitive, so you are probably not surprised that I made my way to the assistant manager and asked how they could be lit up in a city of darkness. He replied: "When we built this hotel, we designed it to also run with a gas generator. We have power on the inside that is not dependent on provisions from the outside." I'm sure that gas generator and all the inner workings came at no small expense, but the owners of this hotel knew it would be worth it in a city this size. They were prepared when everyone around them was not. As a result, they experienced peace in the midst of sudden chaos.

If you haven't noticed, things are getting dark all around us. In every direction you look, our society has become dark. Darkness prevails in every direction. Similar to the total solar eclipse, whose totality passed through my home state of Texas not too long ago, darkness engulfs us even in the middle of the day. As our secular society devolves into the totality of darkness, which we witness deep shadows of right now, we need to solidify our spiritual state so we can withstand the chaos ahead.

Millions of people traveled to Texas and the surrounding states to witness the solar eclipse. The National Guard was called up and several governors issued states of emergency so they would be prepared. When an infrastructure is not built to sustain an influx of millions of visitors, backup resources need to be arranged ahead of time. That's why it's critical to be prepared. It's critical to plan now for the increase in darkness to come.

There's a familiar but also a significant sermon in Matthew's gospel that I look to for guidance and strength for the times we are facing and the times we are about to face. We often refer to it as the Sermon on the Mount. This sermon summarizes the values of the kingdom of God. I go into greater detail on this sermon in much of my preaching, but for our purposes in this book, I want to summarize the Beatitudes for you. When you and I learn to apply the rules of the realm of God in the locale of earth, we tap into a greater unleashing of God's work in and through us than we ever knew was possible.

In this sermon, Jesus spoke on the core, recognizable expectations of what it means to be a kingdom follower. He talked about what kingdom followers ought to prioritize and hold dear, as well as what they should portray to the world around them. Living according to the principles in this sermon not only brings light to a dark world, but it also brings us personal blessing and spiritual power. It's a win-win for everyone.

UNDERSTANDING TRUE BLESSINGS

An interesting thing I want to point out before we dive into these key spiritual principles is the full definition of the word *blessed*. Since the word *blessed* (Greek *makarios*) shows up nine times in this sermon, it's important to examine it fully. The term *blessed* was related to an island off the coast of Greece that was known as Makarios during Jesus' lifetime. The reason why this island was known as the blessed island was due to its self-sufficiency. Like the Marriott lit up in New York City during the blackout, Makarios did not rely on outside power to keep it running well. It had all it needed to fully sustain its inhabitants.

To be blessed is to have all you need. It's a concept of divine favor where the provision of God flows both to you and through you with ease. To live the blessed life as a believer in Jesus Christ is to recognize Him as your Source and tap into His provision spiritually, emotionally, and physically. But many people confuse the term *blessing* as being only about what you receive. They forget that it has more to do with others than themselves.

When God provides a blessing, He gives it to you so you

can share it with others. The island of Makarios was self-sufficient because no one person used up the resources. The resources on the island were available to all the people there. If and when you use your blessings only for yourself, you are no longer living according to kingdom principles. Genesis 12:2 displays this for us: "And I will make you a great nation, and I will bless you, and make your name great; and so you shall be a blessing."

The concept of a biblical blessing involves divine favor, which is the goodness of God flowing in you so it can also flow through you. The moment you become a cul-de-sac Christian rather than a neighborhood-BBQ saint is the moment you start to self-limit your blessings. God is not going to continue to bless a self-centered saint. Knowing this, you can see how it would be wise to let God know how you plan to use the blessings He gives you in order to help others. When you go to God in prayer, asking for something from Him, be sure to let Him know how it will also benefit someone else. You are blessed to be a blessing, which is why it is more blessed to give than to receive (Acts 20:35).

THE PRINCIPLES FOUND IN THE SERMON ON THE MOUNT

Unleashing God's work in your life comes through living according to the principles in the Sermon on the Mount. In Matthew 5, when Jesus said that you are blessed, He intended that blessing to flow through you to others. Let's look at these principles now.

When you go to God in prayer, asking for something from Him, be sure to let Him know how it will also benefit someone else. You are blessed to be a blessing, which is why it is more blessed to give than to receive.

The Principle of Dependence

Jesus began by saying, "Blessed are the poor in spirit, for theirs is the kingdom of heaven" (Matthew 5:3). To be "poor in spirit" describes people who recognize their own insufficiency. They recognize they don't have enough on their own. Those who are poor in spirit understand their own lack. They are self-aware concerning their need for God and His provision. Spiritual insufficiency means that if God doesn't do it, help you in it, provide for it, then you won't have enough to complete it on your own.

The moment you have become self-sufficient in your own mind, you have positioned yourself as God's enemy. I say that because pride is at the heart of self-sufficiency, and pride is the sin of the devil. In fact, one of the most mentioned sins in Scripture is pride. Satan fell and rebelled when he chose to no longer be dependent upon God. Satan wanted to be independent. He wanted to make it without God. Yet a person who is poor in spirit recognizes, in humility, what Jesus said to be true, "Apart from Me you can do nothing" (John 15:5).

God loves dependent followers. To depend upon Him doesn't nullify your own gifts, abilities, and resources; it just shifts your focus from yourself to Him as your Source. When you recognize your insufficiency apart from Him, you receive the gift of the kingdom of heaven. That means God will give you the rule of the kingdom of heaven to operate in your life. Keep in mind, heaven's rule overrules whatever happens on earth. Thus, if you choose to be dependent upon earth for your needs, God will let you handle it on your own.

But if you choose to be dependent upon God for your needs, He gives you the gift of heaven's rule on earth.

The Principle of Mourning

Second in Christ's sermon, He told us that we unleash the blessings of heaven when we mourn: "Blessed are those who mourn, for they shall be comforted" (Matthew 5:4). There are many ways people interpret this verse, but I want to summarize it like this: You are blessed when what hurts the heart of God hurts your heart too. You are blessed when you feel about evil the way God feels about evil. You are blessed when you mourn your own failures and sin because you know you have failed God and God hates sin (James 4:8–10). For example, when Lazarus died and Jesus saw the effects of sin that brought about death in the world, He wept (John 11:35). Jesus wept when He experienced firsthand the ripple effects of the destruction sin brings about.

The way to unleash God's comfort in your heart, soul, and circumstances is to mourn the things that grieve the Lord. God will comfort you when He sees you hurt over the things that hurt Him.

The effects of sin, whether through selfishness, indulgences, apathy, greed, or something else, destroy people's lives. When you see all of this taking place in our world—as we witness the rise of crime, vitriol, hatred, racism, classism, and more—it ought to cause your heart to mourn. The result of this mourning is to receive the comfort of Christ.

I know when I lost my wife Lois to cancer, comfort was something I needed and accepted. Not only comfort from Christ but also comfort from others. We all need comfort at different stages in our lives. The way to unleash God's comfort in your heart, soul, and circumstances is to mourn the things that grieve the Lord. God will comfort you when He sees you hurt over the things that hurt Him. Just like a mother who comforts her child who is sitting in a dirty diaper, God comforts His children when they cry out to Him due to the presence of sin in their lives.

The Principle of Meekness

In His sermon, Jesus went on to say, "Blessed are the gentle, for they shall inherit the earth" (Matthew 5:5). Some translations say, "Blessed are the meek." Now, keep in mind, meek does not mean weak. The best way to understand biblical meekness is by looking at a wild horse. The average horse weighs more than a thousand pounds. When a cowboy tries to break the horse in order to ride it, the horse will fight back. Eventually, if the cowboy knows what he is doing and climbs back on when he is bucked off, the horse learns to trust and respond to him. Once it's broken, the horse uses its strength under the control of someone else. The horse doesn't lose its strength. The horse can still run as fast as it ever could. But now it responds to the leading and guidance of another.

To live a life of biblical meekness means to surrender to the will, leading, and guidance of God. It means to no longer resist the will of God. Gentleness involves surrender and trust. It involves letting God lead. It involves faith. Moses is called the meekest man who ever lived (Numbers 12:3 KJV). Because he lived with a spirit of gentleness, God showed up for him when he needed Him to do so. In fact, just a couple of verses after we are told that Moses is the meekest man who ever lived, we see God interjecting Himself into a scenario in order to defend Moses.

> Then the LORD came down in a pillar of cloud and stood at the doorway of the tent, and He called Aaron and Miriam. When they had both come forward, He said,
>
> > "Hear now My words:
> > If there is a prophet among you,
> > I, the Lord, shall make Myself known to him
> > in a vision.
> > I shall speak with him in a dream.
> > Not so, with My servant Moses,
> > he is faithful in all My household;
> > with him I speak mouth to mouth,
> > even openly, and not in dark sayings,
> > and he beholds the form of the Lord.
> > Why then were you not afraid
> > to speak against My servant, against Moses?"
>
> So the anger of the Lord burned against them and He departed. But when the cloud had withdrawn from over the tent, behold, Miriam was leprous, as white as snow.

As Aaron turned toward Miriam, behold, she was leprous. (vv. 5–10)

Once Aaron and Miriam came out against Moses for marrying an Ethiopian woman with dark skin, God entered the situation as Moses' defender. He did this because Moses was meek. Far too often people have to defend themselves because they fail to surrender to the will of God. Thus, God does not feel obligated to intervene in the earthly situation. It is the meek who shall inherit divine intervention on earth.

We are called and created to live all of life under the rule of God. Those who surrender humbly to God will inherit all He has in store for them on earth.

An inheritance will often come with conditions. Suppose a wealthy person's child was strung out on drugs; the will of the wealthy person may specify the inheritance cannot go to him or her while they are addicted. Every Christian has an inheritance that God is determined to make available to them. But a lot of believers' inheritances are still hanging out in the heavens because they have failed to satisfy the conditions. One condition is to live a gentle, humble, and meek life. In short, we are called and created to live all of life under the rule of God. Those who surrender humbly to God will inherit all He has in store for them on earth.

The Principle of Righteousness

Another way to unleash God's blessings in your experiences is to hunger after God. We read, "Blessed are those who hunger and thirst for righteousness, for they shall be satisfied" (Matthew 5:6). Jesus was talking about a spiritual appetite. While the body needs food, the soul needs righteousness. Righteousness has to do with doing that which pleases God. When the soul consumes righteousness regularly, your life becomes satiated, satisfied. The reason we have so many dissatisfied people is because we have so many spiritually hungry people. If you feed your soul with that which the world has to offer, you will stay spiritually hungry.

When I travel, I try to eat wisely. It's easier to do so at home within the boundaries of life's routine. But when you travel and go to so many different restaurants that offer so many different delicious options, it's easy to eat less wisely. The problem isn't that my hunger has increased when I travel. My hunger is the same. The problem is that what they are offering at all the various restaurants tastes so good. And because it tastes so good, I want to eat more than my fair share at times.

When Christians choose to travel the kingdom of this world and try out the various dishes the culture and society serve up, they may find them to taste good. But like a doughnut tastes good yet has no nutritional value, what society offers the soul has no spiritual value. There is a difference between what your soul wants and what your soul needs in order to be satisfied. You unleash the blessings of satisfaction in your life when you learn to hunger and thirst for righteousness.

Everyone has an appetite. The question is this: What are you hungry for? I passed a homeless man not long ago who had a sign that said "Hungry." I rolled down my window and asked him if he wanted me to get him something to eat. He said no. I was confused. His sign said he was hungry. That's when he told me I could give him some money to get it himself. What he was hungry and thirsty for wasn't necessarily what his body needed.

Similarly, when our soul is stained by the world and its ways, we begin to hunger and thirst for that which is not good for us. Feeding on the flesh of this world will only lead to dissatisfaction. Hungering after God's righteousness unleashes true satisfaction within.

The Principle of Mercy

Jesus went on in His sermon with the next way to unleash blessings, which is through showing other people mercy. He said, "Blessed are the merciful, for they shall receive mercy" (Matthew 5:7). Mercy involves undeserved compassion, along with relief from suffering. Mercy is designed to relieve misery. It's also called upon to forgive or offer a reprieve from negative consequences that you deserve. If a police officer pulls you over, I'm sure you are hoping that she shows you mercy. You probably breathe a sigh of relief when you are told you are getting only a warning this time. Mercy is the visible expression of compassion.

It's easier to ask for mercy than it is to show it. But Jesus reminded us in this verse that we receive mercy from God by showing mercy to others. When it comes time for us to ask for God's mercy in our lives, He checks our mercy account to see what we have done or not done for others. Many people who want mercy are unwilling to give it. But God's blessings are often conditional, and in order to receive mercy, you need to show mercy.

Luke 6:38 describes the conditional nature of many of God's blessings: "Give, and it will be given to you. They will pour into your lap a good measure—pressed down, shaken together, and running over. For by your standard of measure it will be measured to you in return." The word *it* in that verse is critical. We are to give the "it" we want to receive. If you want mercy unleashed upon you, give mercy to others by helping to relieve their misery.

The Principle of Purity

Jesus followed up His statement on mercy with another blessing. He told us that we are blessed if we have pure hearts: "Blessed are the pure in heart, for they shall see God" (Matthew 5:8). The pure in heart are the authentic, undivided, nonduplicitous believers who pursue God with a full commitment. These individuals love from a pure soul, not for dishonest gain. They refrain from manipulation or control. They seek to honor God in what they say and do because they love Him, not because they want something from Him.

Those with a pure heart get to see God. They unleash the ability to see the spiritual, behind the veil. They see His shekinah glory. Since God is Spirit and does not exist in a physical form, His shekinah glory is where He manifests His presence visibly. Like the fire that led the Israelites through the wilderness, God can show up in ways we can see in our physical reality. Those who are pure in heart get to see more of God in their circumstances. They won't have to depend on someone else's testimony because they personally will be able to see God and His divine intervention for themselves.

The Principle of Seeking Peace

Jesus continued in His sermon with another blessing. This time He referred to the blessing given to those who seek peace. He called them peacemakers: "Blessed are the peacemakers, for they shall be called sons of God" (Matthew 5:9). Peacemakers are those people who seek to resolve conflict and reestablish broken relationships. They are bridge builders, not bridge destroyers.

In a culture built on division and sustained by constant warring among factions and groups, it is important that we, as Christians, seek peace. When conflict rears its ugly head, we are to be the ones who step up to pursue peace and harmony. The call of the cross of Jesus Christ is a call to reconcile people to Him and to one another, not to divide. When you live according to this kingdom principle, you will be blessed with being called the sons of God. In other words, you will receive public recognition. God will make sure you are not ignored or marginalized in relationship to Him. You will be known as His child.

The call of the cross of Jesus Christ is a call to reconcile people to Him and to one another, not to divide.

The Principle of Blessings Through Sacrifice

Finally, Jesus concluded His Sermon on the Mount with the blessing of a heavenly reward. This blessing might raise some eyebrows because it comes with a bit of a sting at the start. To unleash a future heavenly reward, though, it requires sacrifice while on earth.

> "Blessed are those who have been persecuted for the sake of righteousness, for theirs is the kingdom of heaven.
>
> "Blessed are you when people insult you and persecute you, and falsely say all kinds of evil against you because of Me. Rejoice and be glad, for your reward in heaven is great; for in the same way they persecuted the prophets who were before you." (Matthew 5:10–12)

When you are rejected because of a righteous stand or when people insult you because you are known as God's child, you get the blessing of a heavenly reward. Living as a Christian does not mean everyone will think great things about you. Living as a Christian means you may face insults and persecution, particularly in the day and age we live in right now. We are living in not only a post-Christian era but an anti-Christian era. If you choose to hold to a biblical standard based on righteousness, you will face rejection at some point. You may even fall victim to the cancel culture. But Jesus reminds you to be glad when this happens because your reward in heaven will be great.

God wants to unleash His blessings in your life whether in the present experience or in the future heavenly experience, but He's looking for those who live according to His kingdom standards. In many ways, that should make you feel good, knowing that you have a direct impact on unleashing God's blessings to you and through you. You have more influence on your own blessings than you possibly thought. If you will strive to live according to these principles found in the Sermon on the Mount, you'll soon discover what it looks and feels like to live the satisfied and blessed Christian life.

Chapter Ten

LEAVING A MARK THAT LASTS

Kingdom Impact

THE SPANISH CIVIL WAR OF 1936–1939 WAS A HIGHLY DEStructive war in Europe, as most wars are. General Emilio Mola led his troops into Madrid at the start of the war hoping for a quick victory. When asked which of his four divisions would be successful in securing the capital city for the Nationalists against the Republicans, he replied that none of them would. Rather, he was relying on a new division, or column, of soldiers embedded deep within the fabric of existing structures. He termed this new column a "fifth column."[1] In the fifth column, strategy was carried out by journalists, businessmen, civilians, and even politicians who held to the Nationalists' view but operated within the Republican realms of the city itself.

These key individuals would seek to secure a victory from within, enabling the four military columns external to Madrid to have an easier time overtaking the city. The siege of Madrid lasted for more than two years until General Mola, along with General Francisco Franco, achieved their goal of taking the city on March 27, 1939.[2]

What's interesting about this concept of the fifth column is that it involved people who were already embedded in enemy territory. They had infiltrated the environment of Madrid so that when the other four columns showed up, the stage had already been set for their entrance. In essence, the fifth column pulled back the curtain to welcome the remaining four columns in to conduct battle. Subsequent to the introduction of this new war strategy, the term *fifth column* was used to refer to individuals in a foreign situation who acted on behalf of their own loyalties. They operated on behalf of a country other than the country they were within. It's a strategy that still works well to this day.

God has an embedded group of fifth columnists as well. These are His kingdom representatives who have been saved, not only for the purpose of going to heaven when they die, but also for representing and advancing God's kingdom agenda on earth. As a reminder, the kingdom agenda can be defined as the visible manifestation of the comprehensive rule of God over every area of life. In short, the kingdom agenda involves God's will revealed in real-time situations. Advancing His kingdom agenda means intentionally committing your time, talents, and treasures to the revelation of His will on earth. It means living out "Your kingdom come. Your will be done, on earth as it is in heaven" (Matthew 6:10).

You and I joined this representative group of kingdom followers once we trusted in Jesus Christ for our personal salvation. We have been redeemed from a place of darkness and sin into the marvelous light of Christ for the purpose of representing heaven in earth's history and, eventually, upon our death, eternity. Our role involves a resistance to cultural norms: refusing to be co-opted by the trends of today and instead representing kingdom values in all we say and do. We are specifically designated to serve heaven's interests in the midst of a secular, declining, and evil society.

Far too many believers have sold out to society. They are owned by a set of values contrary to God's kingdom.

The problem arises, though, when many of us get bought out by the culture. Far too many believers have sold out to society. They are owned by a set of values contrary to God's kingdom values, so much so that they are no longer representing the kingdom of God. They are instead Benedict Arnolds of God's kingdom. This causes great confusion when people look to believers to live out the principles of the kingdom, but believers fail to do so.

LIVING AS A KINGDOM REPRESENTATIVE

Jesus reflected on this gifting of kingdom authority to His disciples in Luke 22:28–30: "You are those who have stood by Me in My trials; and just as My Father has granted Me a kingdom, I grant you that you may eat and drink at My table in My kingdom, and you will sit on thrones judging the twelve tribes of Israel."

The kingdom responsibility handed to Jesus to manifest on earth was then shared to those He granted to eat and drink at His table in His kingdom. As His followers, we also have the ability to tap into this kingdom authority and unleash it in our lives. Looking to the disciples as a model, we can find out what it means to live as a kingdom representative in culture. The apostle Peter provided us with great insights on kingdom living and our purpose on earth:

> Therefore, putting aside all malice and all deceit and hypocrisy and envy and all slander, like newborn babies, long for the pure milk of the word, so that by it you may grow in respect to salvation, if you have tasted the kindness of the Lord.
>
> And coming to Him as to a living stone which has been rejected by men, but is choice and precious in the sight of God, you also, as living stones, are being built up

as a spiritual house for a holy priesthood, to offer up spiritual sacrifices acceptable to God through Jesus Christ. For this is contained in Scripture:

"Behold, I lay in Zion a choice stone, a precious corner stone,

and he who believes in Him will not be disappointed."

This precious value, then, is for you who believe; but for those who disbelieve,

"The stone which the builders rejected,

this became the very corner stone,"

and,

"A stone of stumbling and a rock of offense";

for they stumble because they are disobedient to the word, and to this doom they were also appointed.

But you are a chosen race, a royal priesthood, a holy nation, a people for God's own possession, so that you may proclaim the excellencies of Him who has called you out of darkness into His marvelous light; for you once were not a people, but now you are the people of God; you had not received mercy, but now you have received mercy. (1 Peter 2:1–10)

Peter made a point to address his readers specifically. He called them a "chosen race" and a "royal priesthood." In using two descriptive terms in "royal priesthood," Peter married two concepts. Royalty has to do with kingship. Priesthood has to do with duty to God. A priest serves as an intermediary between God and man.

Peter followed up these descriptions by reminding his

readers that they are owned by God. He said we are "a people for God's own possession." No other place in Scripture does a better job of outlining our purpose and explaining why we are here on earth. We have been chosen to reflect and represent God's kingdom on earth under His rule and sovereignty. When you and I do that, we unleash all He has in store to support the advancement of His kingdom.

This reality ought to change how we show up in life. Far too many believers live an "under the circumstances" sort of existence. But when you realize you are chosen, appointed, and supplied with all you need to carry out God's kingdom authority on earth, it ought to change your perspective not only toward yourself but also toward your circumstances.

We are always to operate in this world according to our identity in Jesus Christ. Peter knew this firsthand because he had confused his race and identity when he refused to eat with the Gentiles (Galatians 2:11–16). He and the other disciples carried out racist actions that Paul called them out on. In fact, Paul told them they had embarrassed the gospel by their actions in failing to honor others as equals. The gospel does not discriminate based on race. Paul reminded them who they were and whose they were when he said, "I have been crucified with Christ; and it is no longer I who live, but Christ lives in me; and the life which I now live in the flesh I live by faith in the Son of God, who loved me and gave Himself up for me" (Galatians 2:20).

Paul wanted Peter to understand that he was a Christian first, not a Jew first. Everything else was to be subjected to his identity in Jesus Christ and Christ's kingdom values. Whatever gets in the way of your honoring Christ and His kingdom principles becomes an impediment to unleashing His presence in your life. We are to live as Christians first, not as Americans first or as our racial identity first or political affiliation first. Far too many believers live powerless Christian lives because they fail to understand this basic foundational life principle. If and when you do not know who you are and whose you are, the Enemy will seek to redefine you according to his goals, strategies, and values. As a result, you will live a double-minded and confused existence, accomplishing little for yourself, God's kingdom, and the greater good of all.

HEAVENLY CITIZENSHIP ON EARTH

Paul emphasized this reality again in Philippians 3:20: "For our citizenship is in heaven, from which also we eagerly wait for a Savior, the Lord Jesus Christ." Jesus isn't handing out dual-citizenship opportunities. He wants you to know that you are a citizen of heaven on a visa to earth. You are simply passing through this land, because your homeland is above. Yet once you forget this, you will easily become too attached to earth, even to the point that the world's wisdom and values will influence your decisions. In short, the world, not God, will own you.

Jesus isn't handing out dual-citizenship opportunities. He wants you to know that you are a citizen of heaven on a visa to earth.

As a citizen of heaven, your allegiance is to God. The principles of God's kingdom are to guide, govern, and goad you in the direction that advances His kingdom purposes. When the culture's priorities disagree or conflict with God's priorities, you are to pursue God's priorities. No matter how much you love and enjoy this world, you will only unleash God's power both in and through you when you align yourself under His overarching rule. Paul described the behavior of those who have sold out to this world order in the verses preceding the one we just read. In Philippians 3:18–19, he said, "For many walk, of whom I often told you, and now tell you even weeping, that they are enemies of the cross of Christ, whose end is destruction, whose god is their appetite, and whose glory is in their shame, who set their minds on earthly things."

Make no mistake about it, your feet are to be firmly planted in the ground as you live your life, but your mind, soul, and spirit are to get life instructions from heaven. You are to draw information from above to execute on earth below. In other words, you are under new management. You are no longer under the domain of darkness or the rules of demons. You are now under the ultimate kingdom authority of Jesus Christ. And just as you would never function by the standard operating procedures of a former place of employment at your new place of employment, you are to no longer function according to Satan's methods and goals. The kingdom of darkness does not dictate to you anymore. At best, Satan can deceive and manipulate you, but he holds no legitimate authority over you.

You must hold fast to the truth that you are special. You are chosen. You are royalty. You are priestly. You live with full access to kingdom authority. What the world wants to do is to deceive you and convince you that you are worthless, inconsequential, and inadequate. But you are worth far more than you ever imagined, and God has created you with all you need to live out His purpose for your life. Jesus Christ and His kingdom is to transcend all else on earth, and this starts with kingdom representatives obediently following Him in their everyday existence.

BECOMING A KINGDOM INFLUENCER

You are a kingdom disciple living as a kingdom servant while making a kingdom impact that will resonate throughout all time. And you do this through what we read earlier from 1 Peter, which says we are to "proclaim the excellencies of Him who has called you out of darkness into His marvelous light" (2:9). You are to be a proclaimer of Christ. A more contemporary term would be *kingdom influencer.* You are to use your status, time, talent, and treasures to influence others for God's glory and the greater good of all. You are to serve notice on the culture that Jesus Christ is here and His kingdom is alive and well. As a kingdom influencer, your intention should be that of proclaiming the gospel to a lost world and bringing glory to God.

Paul outlined this mission of ours as kingdom influencers in 2 Corinthians 5:16–21:

You are a kingdom disciple living as a kingdom servant while making a kingdom impact that will resonate throughout all time.

> Therefore from now on we recognize no one according to the flesh; even though we have known Christ according to the flesh, yet now we know Him in this way no longer. Therefore if anyone is in Christ, he is a new creature; the old things passed away; behold, new things have come. Now all these things are from God, who reconciled us to Himself through Christ and gave us the ministry of reconciliation, namely, that God was in Christ reconciling the world to Himself, not counting their trespasses against them, and He has committed to us the word of reconciliation.
>
> Therefore, we are ambassadors for Christ, as though God were making an appeal through us; we beg you on behalf of Christ, be reconciled to God. He made Him who knew no sin to be sin on our behalf, so that we might become the righteousness of God in Him.

Paul called us "ambassadors" (v. 20). *Ambassador* is another term for representative or influencer. In the political realm, an ambassador is someone who has been duly deputized to go to another country and represent their homeland. They hold an official title and responsibility to represent the nation they've been sent out from. Thus, ambassadors sent from the United States are not promoting the culture of foreign lands as their primary goal. They are to promote the values and prosperity of the United States of America.

Paul called each of us an ambassador who has been saved by Jesus Christ. As I've noted, our job is to take the values of the kingdom of heaven and promote them in the culture of this world. Whether this is on the job, in the marketplace, to family members, in your community, or even in your church doesn't matter. What matters is that you promote God's kingdom principles everywhere you are.

The moment the culture disagrees with God's principles, you are to disagree with the culture. You are not an ambassador of earth. You are an ambassador of the kingdom of heaven. Heaven's values are to inform your words, worldview, concepts, and actions. They are to inform every aspect of your life because you are a citizen from on high. To acquiesce to the culture negates the purpose and effectiveness of your true role.

Unfortunately, God has a lot of His followers keeping the title but failing to carry out the role. They are not representing the kingdom of God in the culture of the world. Rather than repenting and returning to God when they veer off course, they have gotten comfortable with society and its ways. Thus they have become useless in advancing God's kingdom agenda on earth.

The question you need to ask yourself as we reach the end of our time together in this book is this: *Am I a kingdom influencer?* Are you making a difference through your influence on others or are you simply promoting the culture at large and its values? Are you standing with the fifth columnists who are seeking to bring about radical transformational change or are you seeking to settle for the status quo? The way you answer those questions will quickly tell you how much of God's kingdom power you are unleashing in your life. God equips and provides for those who live according to His purposes. He has never stated that He will equip and provide for those who are apathetic to His kingdom cause.

GRATITUDE AND SERVICE IN GOD'S KINGDOM

When your Christianity is visible, you'll effect change. You'll unleash kingdom authority. You'll live as a kingdom influencer making a difference. You must live as a visible, verbal follower of Jesus Christ, not as a secret-agent Christian. Now, you are to do this lovingly and with compassion and sensitivity, but you are to stand for what you know to be true. You are not to be ashamed of the gospel. You are not to be ashamed of God's taking you out of darkness and placing you in the light. As Peter wrote, you are to "keep your behavior excellent among the Gentiles, so that in the thing in which they slander you as evildoers, they may because of your good deeds, as they observe them, glorify God in the day of visitation" (1 Peter 2:12).

People should see your good works and hear your good words. You need to live with both verbalizations and demonstrations of God's kingdom power. Good works are biblically authorized activity that bring benefit to others in the name of the Lord. We are to live in ways that let others see the love of God and draw nearer to Him as a result.

God is looking for His own CIA team—Christians in Action. He's looking for Christians who demonstrate through their actions that He is King over all. He wants others to see that Christians are kind, good people and they represent

His kingdom well. God wants kingdom influencers who will serve Him out of a heart of gratitude. The psalmist penned this as serving the Lord with gladness.

> Shout joyfully to the Lord, all the earth.
> Serve the Lord with gladness;
> come before Him with joyful singing.
> Know that the Lord Himself is God;
> it is He who has made us, and not we
> ourselves;
> we are His people and the sheep of His
> pasture.
> Enter His gates with thanksgiving
> and His courts with praise.
> Give thanks to Him, bless His name.
> For the Lord is good;
> His lovingkindness is everlasting
> and His faithfulness to all generations.
> (Psalm 100:1–5)

We shouldn't be pouting when it comes to showing up as God's kingdom representatives. We shouldn't be serving God with a sour attitude. God desires to have smiling servants who serve Him with humble hearts. To help you understand this more clearly, let me give you an illustration. Let's say you were at a restaurant and your waiter showed up with an attitude. After you sat down, the waiter took longer than normal to come to your table. Then, when he got there, he said abruptly, "What do you want?" He didn't give you time to decide. He didn't offer to come back if you needed more time. He just demanded you order right then.

After taking your order, let's say the waiter then brought your food and set it down in any location on your table. He didn't put it in front of the person who ordered it. He didn't even put it within reach. He just dropped it off as quickly as possible and then left. I bet you wouldn't go back to that restaurant again. What's more, you wouldn't leave a tip. And I've got a feeling there are some of you who would leave a bad online review as well. This is because when you go to a restaurant, you expect excellent service. Restaurants aren't cheap, especially these days. So if you are going to support a restaurant, you expect the service will reflect the best industry standards.

As a kingdom representative, Jesus has paid the price for your service. He doesn't want you serving Him with a bad attitude or a complaining spirit. We are to "serve the LORD with gladness." Not only that, but we are to serve out of a heart of thankfulness. It's easy to thank someone who hands you some change after you pay your bill or someone who opens a door for you. We know to do this as a courtesy response. But we have forgotten to thank God for the myriad provisions and blessings He gives us daily. Everything in life that you possess is a gift from God. Our thanks should be ongoing and automatic. You should be thanking Him all day long. Thank Him that you woke up today. Thank Him that you are not starving. Thank Him for every moment He has supplied. If you have a car, thank Him for it. If you have a job, thank Him for it.

In other words, consider what the Lord has done for you, and when you do, serve Him from a heart of thanksgiving. When you do, you'll discover that bringing joy to God's heart unleashes even more blessings in your life. God hangs out in the environment and atmosphere of our praise. Thus, when you praise Him, you are inviting Him into a closer proximity with you.

It's easy to thank God for the big stuff, but if God didn't consistently supply the regular things we need in our lives, the big stuff couldn't come into our lives either. We need to thank God for everything and then allow that spirit of gratitude to propel us to serve Him as His kingdom representatives. Giving thanks lets God know you are thinking about Him. It lets God know you haven't gotten a big head and started thinking that you are the source for your life. It lets God know that He's important to you and that you recognize every good thing comes from Him. When you acknowledge God's place in your life through praise and service, you invite Him to unleash His goodness even more.

God wants to do great things both in you and through you. These things are intended to benefit you but also to benefit those you come into contact with. Yet He's waiting on you to fulfill the conditions of these blessings from above. He's waiting on you to walk by faith in a spirit of humility, gratitude, and trust.

Serving God means staying in close contact with Him so you can hear Him and know what to do and say every moment. It means drawing near to Him in order to tap into His grace, majesty, and power. Living as a kingdom influencer requires you to wear His brand and reflect His image to others. When you do that, He will empower you to be seen and recognized by others as His follower. His kingdom power is closer to you than you may think. What's more, He's given you the insight into what it takes to access it. Doing so is up to you. God has made His kingdom blessings, grace, and might available to you.

In fact, the kingdom of God is at hand. Or, rather, the kingdom of God is in your hands. It's up to you to unleash it.

APPENDIX

THE URBAN ALTERNATIVE

At the Urban Alternative (TUA), our mission is simple: equip, empower, and unite believers to impact lives, families, churches, and communities through a kingdom agenda worldview. We believe that the root of today's problems—personal, societal, and even within the church—is spiritual. That means the solution isn't found in politics, economics, or empty religion but in God's kingdom rule over every area of life.

WHAT IS THE KINGDOM AGENDA?

The kingdom agenda is the visible manifestation of the comprehensive rule of God over every area of life. The Bible isn't just a collection of inspiring stories—it's a unified blueprint for advancing God's glory and His kingdom from Genesis to Revelation. When we grasp this, we realize that God's rule isn't just for the past—it's for right now.

Too many of us keep God at a distance—close enough for emergencies but not central to daily life. But true transformation happens when we bring God "downtown" into the core of who we are.

When we align ourselves under God's rule, we experience His power and authority in every area—personal, family, church, and community. As we submit to Him, we don't just touch heaven—we change earth.

WHY DOES IT MATTER?

Without God's kingdom influence, everything crumbles.

People live compartmentalized, divided lives.

Families break down, chasing personal satisfaction instead of purpose.

Churches lose impact, focusing inward instead of outward.

Communities search for answers in all the wrong places.

When we bring God's agenda back to the center, hope is restored. No matter how broken life looks—whether it's relationships, finances, or lost dreams—God sustains, restores, and revives. As long as God is in the picture, it's not over.

HOW WE EQUIP AND IMPACT

Broadcast Media

Millions engage with *The Alternative with Dr. Tony Evans* daily through radio, TV, and digital platforms across 130+ countries. Listen online or download the Tony Evans app.

Personal Training

The Tony Evans Training Center (TETC) offers online and in-person courses in the Bible, theology, leadership, and more. Visit tonyevanstraining.org.

Kingdom Agenda Pastors (KAP) equips pastors with biblical leadership tools. Learn more at kafellowship.org.

Pastors' Wives Ministry, founded by the late Dr. Lois Evans, supports women in ministry. Visit loisevans.org.

Community Transformation

We provide churches with strategies for real impact, from adopting schools to fostering unity with law enforcement. We are committed to uniting believers and churches to bring real transformation through our "Three Point Strategy." Our strategy includes:

Assembling in Unity—Bringing people together across divisions

Addressing Core Issues—Tackling what divides us with biblical truth

Acting for Social Impact—Partnering to transform communities

Want to be part of the movement? Text the word STRATEGY to 55659 or visit tonyevans.org/strategy to get involved.

Tony Evans Films

Through powerful storytelling, Tony Evans Films creates Bible-based movies and documentaries, including *Kingdom Men Rising* and *Journey with Jesus.*

Resource Development

Dr. Tony Evans has published over 150 books and studies, including the first full-Bible commentary and study Bible by an African American, now on display at the Museum of the Bible.

STAY CONNECTED

God's kingdom agenda is the answer our world needs. Whether through teaching, training, or community outreach, TUA is committed to helping you live anchored in Christ.

Stay connected at tonyevans.org or call (800) 800-3222 or text the word DEVO to 55659 to receive Dr. Evans's weekly devotional.

NOTES

Chapter 3

1. Eleanor Bird, "Anxiety Prescriptions on the Rise Among Young Adults," Medical News Today, April 5, 2022, www.medicalnewstoday.com/articles/healthy/anxiety-prescriptions-on-the-rise-among-young-adults.

Chapter 10

1. James M. Markham, "Madrid's 'Fifth Column' Harbors Memory and Hope," *New York Times*, February 7, 1982, www.nytimes.com/1982/02/07/weekinreview/madrid-s-fifth-column-harbors-memory-and-hope.html.
2. John Simkin, "Madrid During the Spanish Civil War," Spartacus Educational, last updated January 2020, https://spartacus-educational.com/SPmadrid.htm.

ABOUT THE AUTHOR

DR. TONY EVANS IS THE FOUNDER AND SENIOR PASTOR OF OAK Cliff Bible Fellowship in Dallas, founder and president of the Urban Alternative, former chaplain of the NBA Dallas Mavericks and the NFL Dallas Cowboys, and author of more than 150 books, booklets, and Bible studies. The first African American to earn a doctorate of theology at Dallas Theological Seminary, he has been named one of the twelve most effective preachers in the English-speaking world by Baylor University.

Dr. Evans holds the honor of writing and publishing the first full-Bible commentary and study Bible by an African

American. His radio broadcast, *The Alternative with Dr. Tony Evans*, can be heard on more than two thousand US outlets daily and in more than 130 countries.

Dr. Evans launched the Tony Evans Training Center (TETC) in 2017, an online learning platform providing quality, seminary-style courses for a fraction of the cost to any person in any place. The TETC currently has over fifty courses to choose from and has a student population of over two thousand.

Dr. Evans was married to Lois, his wife and ministry partner of more than fifty years, until Lois transitioned to glory in late 2019. They are the proud parents of four, grandparents of thirteen, and great-grandparents of four. In November 2023, Dr. Evans married Carla Evans.

For more information, visit tonyevans.org.